2ND EDITION

MALCOLM MCDONALD ON MARKETING PLANNING

UNDERSTANDING MARKETING PLANS AND STRATEGY

MALCOLM MCDONALD

Publisher's note

Every possible effort has been made to ensure that the information contained in this book is accurate at the time of going to press, and the publisher and author cannot accept responsibility for any errors or omissions, however caused. No responsibility for loss or damage occasioned to any person acting, or refraining from action, as a result of the material in this publication can be accepted by the editor, the publisher or the author.

First published in Great Britain in 2002 by Kogan Page Limited entitled *If You're So Brilliant... How Come Your Marketing Plans Aren't Working?*
Reissued in 2008 entitled *Malcolm McDonald on Marketing Planning*
Second edition published in Great Britain and the United States in 2017

2nd Floor, 45 Gee Street
London EC1V 3RS
United Kingdom
www.koganpage.com

MPHC Marketing
122 W 27th St, 10th Floor
New York NY 10001
USA

4737/23 Ansari Road
Daryaganj
New Delhi 110002
India

ISBN 978 0 7494 7821 6
E-ISBN 978 0 7494 7822 3

British Library Cataloguing-in-Publication Data

A CIP record for this book is available from the British Library.

Library of Congress Cataloging-in-Publication Data

Names: McDonald, Malcolm, author.
Title: Malcolm McDonald on marketing planning : understanding marketing plans and strategy / Malcolm McDonald.
Other titles: How come your marketing plans aren't working?
Description: Second edition. | New York : Kogan Page, 2016. | Revised edition of the author's Malcolm McDonald on marketing planning, 2008. | Includes bibliographical references and index.
Identifiers: LCCN 2016037290 (print) | LCCN 2016038888 (ebook) | ISBN 9780749478216 (paperback) | ISBN 9780749478223 (ebook)
Subjects: LCSH: Marketing–Planning. | Marketing–Management. | BISAC: BUSINESS & ECONOMICS / Marketing / General. | BUSINESS & ECONOMICS / Strategic Planning.
Classification: LCC HF5415.13 .M369157 2016 (print) | LCC HF5415.13 (ebook) | DDC 658.8/02–dc23
LC record available at https://lccn.loc.gov/2016037290

Typeset by Graphicraft Limited, Hong Kong
Print production managed by Jellyfish
Printed and bound by CPI Group (UK) Ltd, Croydon, CR0 4YY

PRAIS
MCDONALD ON MARKETING
P

'This excellent book clearly describes how to create winning strategies. As an owner and manager of an SME who has attended Malcolm McDonald's classes and worked with him delivering programmes, I can vouch it works. Major profitable growth can be achieved in a short period, leaving competitors in your wake. This is a must-read for any owners or managers serious about business growth.'
Stewart Barnes, Managing Director, QuoLux

'(Once again) Professor McDonald has captured the essence of world-class marketing planning which is applicable to both the SME and the MNC. His razor-sharp focus is directed at markets based on the needs of customers and identifying profitable market segments, which, whilst logically intuitive, requires a mindset shift for companies that often focus on forecasts and budgets first in their planning. He takes the reader through a step-by-step process to make these changes in approaching real market understanding and planning to capture value. Highly readable and practical!'
Siobhan McAleer, Commercial Director, Irish Management Institute

'This book is essential reading for all small businesses wanting to write a marketing plan that works effectively across your organization, achieves growth and maximizes commercial profits. For the last 20 years, I have worked with SMEs and venture capitalists, created and sold companies, and now specialize in supporting small enterprises with a marketing strategy that is measured and delivers exceptional return on investment. This book will save business owners consultancy fees (and allow them to ask suppliers the right questions), as well as help marketing agencies and marketers deliver significantly beyond their existing performance.'
Kelvin Golding FCIM, Chartered Institute of Marketing Small Business Ambassador and Regional Chairman

CONTENTS

PREFACE

There can be no doubt that the future prosperity of the UK economy and, indeed, many other Western European economies, will depend on the success of the majority of companies that are not classified as 'multinationals' (MNCs), particularly those that trade outside their home country. As small medium enterprises (SMEs) represent about 95 per cent of all corporate enterprises in the UK and provide over 65 per cent of all employment, throughout this book I will refer to SMEs, even though everything I say applies to all organizations of whatever size and kind.

To succeed as an SME in any market, wherever in the world it is, requires a deep understanding of that market, irrespective of whether you choose to enter via a distributor, a joint venture, or indeed as a wholly owned subsidiary.

The issues faced by all SMEs are:

- whether to sell abroad;
- where to sell abroad;
- how to enter;
- what to sell abroad;
- how to succeed abroad.

This book is NOT about issues 1–3 above. IT IS ABOUT HOW TO SUCCEED ONCE YOU ARE THERE. For example, once you are in France, Germany, Indonesia, or indeed anywhere, to succeed in that market, you will need to do what is spelled out in this book. In particular, you will need to know:

- how the market works from end to end;
- who makes the decisions about what is bought;
- what these decision makers really need;

- how well what you are offering meets these needs compared with competitive offers;
- how to make an offer that creates advantage for customers, so making the price you charge almost irrelevant;
- how to allocate your scarce resources to achieve the best results.

If you can master the above six essential issues, you will no longer be at the beck and call of customers, distributors or any other kind of intermediary, as they will be so thankful to you for creating such profitable business for them.

In short, this book will spell out how to grow your sales and profits to achieve your objectives.

IMPORTANT NOTE TO THE READER OF THIS BOOK – PLEASE READ THIS

I have organized this book in a way that will take you through a logical sequence of steps, the end result of which will be a strategic plan setting out how you will be able to grow your sales and profits to achieve the objectives that you and your colleagues have set.

There is one chapter, however, that is key to success and that is the chapter on market segmentation – Chapter 5.

The reason I am pointing it out now is that in today's commercial world, all organizations have excellent products, so the chance of gaining sustainable competitive advantage from product superiority is extremely limited.

When I ask attendees on my courses all over the world how many have excellent products, every hand goes up. When I ask them how many are short of profitable customers, every hand goes up. The truth is that success comes not from great products, but from differentiation and differentiation comes from the way you relate to your markets and customers.

The most important lesson I have learned from my very long career is that customers love suppliers who understand their business, their problems and their issues rather than suppliers who bowl up trying to sell their products. Suppliers who make offers to customers that create financial advantage for them, rather than offers that merely help them avoid disadvantage, are the suppliers who go from strength to strength.

I don't want you to start reading this book from Chapter 5 onwards. That is not the point I am trying to make, as the first four chapters are crucial in the process of profit-making.

What I do hope you will do, however, is to understand that the most tried and tested route to commercial success is needs-based market segmentation, so please read Chapter 5 carefully.

Thank you.

Let's get real 01

By the end of this chapter, readers will understand:

- The supremacy of customers over products
- Why trading on price is dangerous
- Why a digital strategy is impossible without a robust commercial strategy
- Why cost cutting and fads just don't work
- What the real challenges are facing all organizations today
- What continuously successful companies do to succeed

Introduction

This book is, quite simply, about how to develop a strategy for making lots of money.

I am Chairman of six small medium enterprises (SMEs) and two-thirds of my income comes from abroad. I have also spent the past 30 years working at board level with major multinationals, so I combine the best of the biggest and most successful companies in the world with the best of the world of entrepreneurs and risk-takers.

Accordingly, there is absolutely nothing I will say in this book that I don't have to do myself in my everyday world. So what is the problem?

Let's start with a simple question.

What are your key target markets in order of priority?

Typically, directors list their **products** in answer to this question (for example, Pensions software). I hasten to remind them, however, that

IBM nearly went bankrupt because they thought they were in the mainframe market. Gestetner thought they were in the duplicator market. More recently, Kodak thought they were in the camera market. Nokia thought they were in the phone market, and so on.

I have never known any company go bankrupt because of poor products. They go bankrupt because of a lack of customers.

In all my years as a Professor, I have never known any company go bankrupt because of poor products. They go bankrupt because of a lack of **customers.**

Yes, of the hundreds of SME plans I have read over the years, most witter on about their products. But the world is awash with products. Customers have an abundance of products to choose from and in the main they just don't care and usually will decide which product to buy based on price.

Now let's move to a second simple question.

In your key target markets, what are your company's sources of differential advantage?

My experience is that most companies can't answer these two simple questions. But if the board of directors can't answer them unequivocally, it makes me wonder what they think their role is.

Let's face it, no one needs me to point out that it is only by selling something to someone that money can be made and we need to know who to sell to, what they really need and why they should buy from us rather than someone offering something similar.

So, this book is mainly about this.

Without being able to answer the above questions, **price** comes into the equation and in the next few paragraphs, I want to dispel once and for all the myth that it is the lowest price that gets the business.

Why competing on price is a no-no

Have a quick look at Table 1.1.

Table 1.1 Think very carefully before price discounting

		–5% Discount	–10% Discount
Price	£10	9.50	9.00
Profit	£2	1.50	1.00
Sell	100	133.30	200

This shows the devastating effect that dropping the price has on profits.

Price always has had the biggest impact on the bottom line, followed by costs and followed in third place by sales.

Now have a look at the following in Table 1.2.

Table 1.2 The impact of price on profit

	Start Point	Vol +1%	Costs –1%	Price +1%
Volume	1000	1010	1000	1010
Fixed Costs	400	400	396	400
Variable Costs	500	505	495	500
Profit	100	105	109	110
Turnover	1000	1010	1000	1010
Profit Increase	**0%**	**5%**	**9%**	**10%**

This shows (and there are hundreds of other examples) that price has always had the biggest impact on the bottom line, followed by costs and followed in third place by sales. Why, then, do companies, try to trade on price given the expensive European Union legislation granting social benefits to employees? How can any European company compete on price against the Third World, with their much lower cost base?

A quick look at the diagram in Figure 1.1 will illustrate that dropping price to maintain sales is a recipe for disaster, whereas **creating** superior value for customers is the right way ahead.

Figure 1.1 Two pricing philosophies

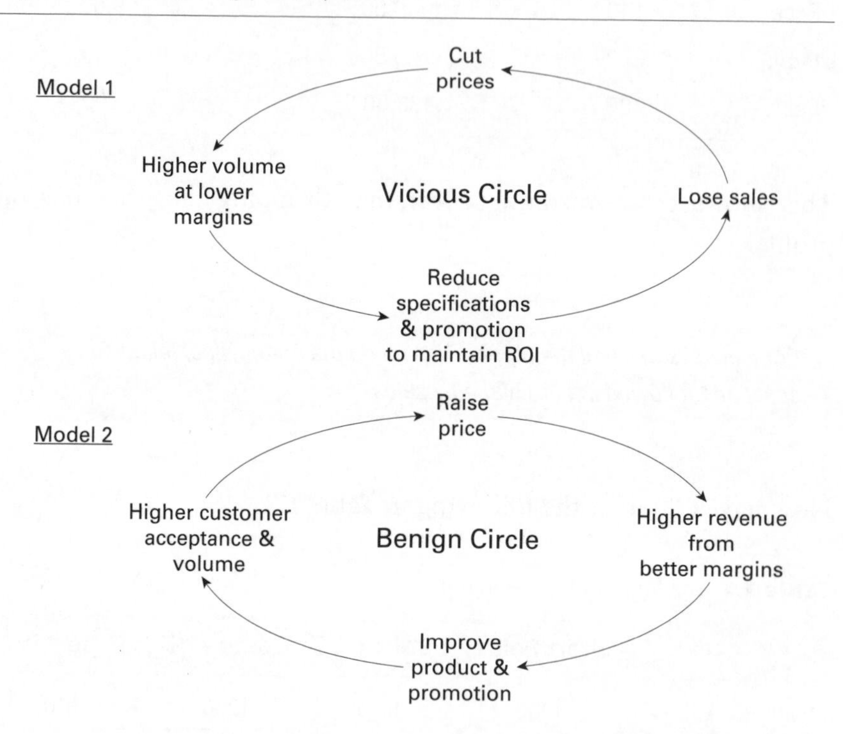

One final point on price. There is much research to show that in every country in the world, the genuine low price segment is never greater than 10 per cent, so it is a real give-away that companies that trade on price only do so because they do not understand the concept of customer value.

Dropping price to maintain sales is a recipe for disaster.

Table 1.3 summarizes the amount of extra sales that have to be made at different margins to compensate for a drop in price.

Table 1.3 Calculator for discount, margin and sales

If you cut your price	and your present gross profit is......							
	5%	10%	15%	20%	25%	30%	35%	40%
	You need to sell this much more to break even......							
	%	%	%	%	%	%	%	%
1%	25.0	11.1	7.1	5.3	4.2	3.4	2.9	2.6
2%	66.6	25.0	15.4	11.1	8.7	7.1	6.1	5.3
3%	150.0	42.0	25.0	17.6	13.6	11.1	9.4	8.1
4%	400.0	66.6	36.4	25.0	19.0	15.4	12.6	11.1
5%	–	100.0	50.0	33.3	25.0	20.0	16.7	14.3
6%	–	150.0	66.7	42.9	31.6	25.0	20.7	17.6
7%	–	233.3	87.5	53.8	38.9	30.4	25.0	21.2
8%	–	400.0	114.3	66.7	47.1	36.4	29.6	25.0
9%	–	1000.0	150.0	81.8	56.3	42.9	34.6	29.0
10%	–	–	200.0	100.0	66.7	50.0	40.0	33.3
11%	–	–	275.0	122.2	78.6	57.9	45.8	37.9
12%	–	–	400.0	150.0	92.3	66.7	52.2	42.9
13%	–	–	650.0	185.7	108.3	76.5	59.1	48.1
14%	–	–	1400.0	233.3	127.3	87.5	66.7	53.8
15%	–	–	–	300.0	150.0	100.0	75.0	60.0
16%	–	–	–	400.0	177.8	114.3	84.2	66.7
17%	–	–	–	566.7	212.5	130.8	94.4	73.9
18%	–	–	–	900.0	257.1	150.0	105.9	81.8
19%	–	–	–	1900.0	316.7	172.7	118.8	90.5
20%	–	–	–	–	400.0	200.0	133.3	100.0
21%	–	–	–	–	525.0	233.0	150.0	110.0
22%	–	–	–	–	733.0	275.0	169.2	122.2
23%	–	–	–	–	1115.0	328.6	191.7	135.3
24%	–	–	–	–	2400.0	400.0	218.2	150.0
25%	–	–	–	–	–	500.0	250.0	166.7

EXAMPLE: Your present gross margin is 25% and you cut your selling price 10%. Locate 10% in the left-hand column. Below, follow across to the column located 25%. You find you will need to sell 66.7% MORE units.

Social media/digital

Next, let's get the social media/digital issue out of the way right at the beginning of this book.

Without a winning strategy for products and markets, it is impossible to have an effective digital strategy.

Almost every course/seminar/workshop today has the word 'digital' in its title. The problem, however, is that unless a company has a robust strategy for what it sells and to whom, it is impossible to have a digital strategy. What makes anyone think that just because a customer is on Facebook, or LinkedIn, that he or she is not the same person as in real life? But without proper, needs-based segmentation (to be addressed in Chapter 5), any digital strategy will be ineffective. There is a well-known cartoon showing the Chief Marketing Officer addressing the board and in answer to the question about why net profits are down by 30 per cent, says: 'Yes, that is a pity, but the good news is that our likes or Facebook have doubled!'

Yes, of course, social media and the like are important, but without a winning strategy for products and markets, it is impossible to have an effective digital strategy. This book, then, is definitely *not* about developing a digital strategy. As I said in the opening sentence, it is about developing a strategy for making lots of money.

A very brief history of management

The diagram in Figure 1.2 illustrates a very brief history of management.

Figure 1.2 A very brief history of management

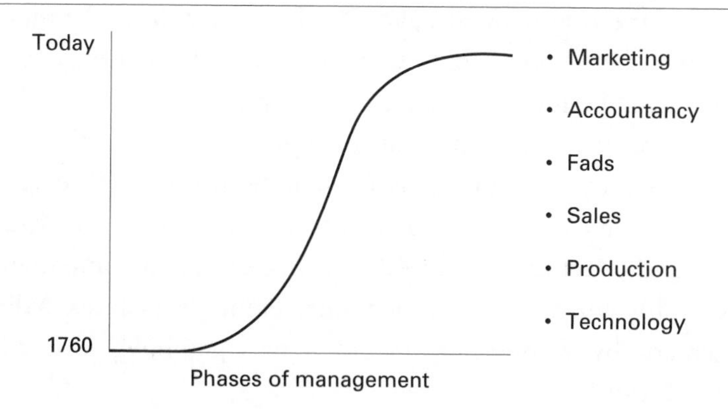

Starting at the bottom left, the first three phases represent technology and production, manifested in the Industrial Revolution, when the agrarian population moved to towns and cities. The exponential growth led to the foundation of the marketing discipline in the form of sales, as people now had a choice.

Cost cutting is finite, whereas value creation for customers in infinite.

Further up the curve, however, it was all to change, as gradually supply grew at a faster rate than demand, with a consequent fall-off of sales and profits, the answer to which was for many years provided by accountants, with their constant rounds of cost cutting, ratio management and the like, most of which, whilst certainly getting rid of unnecessary costs, led to 'Anorexia Industrialosa' (an excessive desire to be leaner and fitter, leading eventually to death!). After all, how many pence are there in a pound (or cents in a euro, or cents in a dollar)? Cost cutting is finite whereas value creation for customers is infinite and is limited only by our creativity and imagination. It was this approach, more than any other that destroyed the UK's industrial supremacy.

It is not well known that, according to David Pearson in *The 20 Ps of Marketing* (Kogan Page, 2014), the UK has 12 times more accountants per capita than Germany. Which economy, we ask, has performed better over the past 65 years?

Next, along came a massive spate of fads to try to rescue the situation, but most of these also failed. For example, no one will ever forget 'In Search of Excellence' by Tom Peters and Robert H Waterman in 1982; or the fact that, of the 43 so-called excellent companies, only six were still considered excellent just eight years later. MBWA – management by wandering around – was genuinely offered as a serious solution!

Others included TQM (Total Quality Management), where anyone could get a certificate as long as they could prove they could make 'crap' perfectly every time! Knowledge Management, Balanced Scorecards, CRM and the like also failed, as did the previous Relationship Marketing fashion.

This movement took on a more open-sandaled hippy view, citing the need to 'delight' our customers.

The problem is, of course, that there is no such thing as a 'customer' and 'delight' is a relative term, depending on which segment customers belong to and what their needs are.

There is no such thing as 'a customer'.

The little story that follows illustrates the point I am trying to make and starts with the example in Figure 1.3.

I was running a sales conference for an international bearings company some years ago, when the CEO stood up and demanded that the sales force should reduce the current 65 debtor days to 45 – more easily said than done in the middle of a recession. The sales force was understandably nervous about this until I explained to them how to do it. I asked them to write the names of their customers on a kind of 'thermometer' (the vertical axis) according to the sales potential of each to give their sales over the next year. They were then asked to put each customer in one of four boxes on a matrix according to whether they 'loved' them or 'hated' them. The lines in each box in Figure 1.3 are the names of customers.

Figure 1.3 The customer matrix

Sales Potential	LOVE	HATE
High		
Low		

I then made the following suggestions:

1 In the bottom-left box, where customers love us but where there is little potential, be nice to them and persuade them to pay in 35 days.

2 In the top-left box, where customers love us and there is potential for sales growth, persuade them to pay in 45 days.

3 In the top-right box, where there is lots of potential but where they 'hate' us, offer them 65 days.

4 One box remains – the bottom-right box – where not only do customers 'hate us', but where there is little potential for growth. For them, if they want to deal with us, they must pay cash – two weeks in advance – and they can come and collect the goods themselves!

Yes, of course this is a ridiculous exaggeration and, given today's rules, may not even be legal, but the example serves to illustrate the point that, depending on the circumstances of different customers, so our commercial policy should be adapted accordingly.

I will explain this in a more sophisticated way in Chapter 5 of this book.

In this example, the bearing company was able to achieve its 45 debtor days on average.

For, now, referring back to Figure 1.2 above, the word 'marketing' appears at the top of the diagram. I must stress, before I go on to explain what the term means, that most of the so-called 'fads' referred to above – the exception being 'In Search of Excellence' – work perfectly well once an organization has a deep understanding of its customers' needs and organizes all its functions around delivering value propositions to satisfy them. Without this, however, all the initiatives referred to above remain expensive and ineffective fads.

Challenges

The three principal challenges facing all organizations today are:

- Market maturity
- Globalization
- Customer power.

For growth today, it is necessary to take share from another competitor.

Another quick look at Figure 1.2 shows a levelling out of demand in most markets. In the West, most people have cars, dishwashers, washing machines, etc, and any expansion is dependent on population growth. This means rate rather than expecting natural growth, it is necessary to take share from competitors, which is where marketing comes in – to be discussed in Chapter 2.

Figure 1.4 Globalization

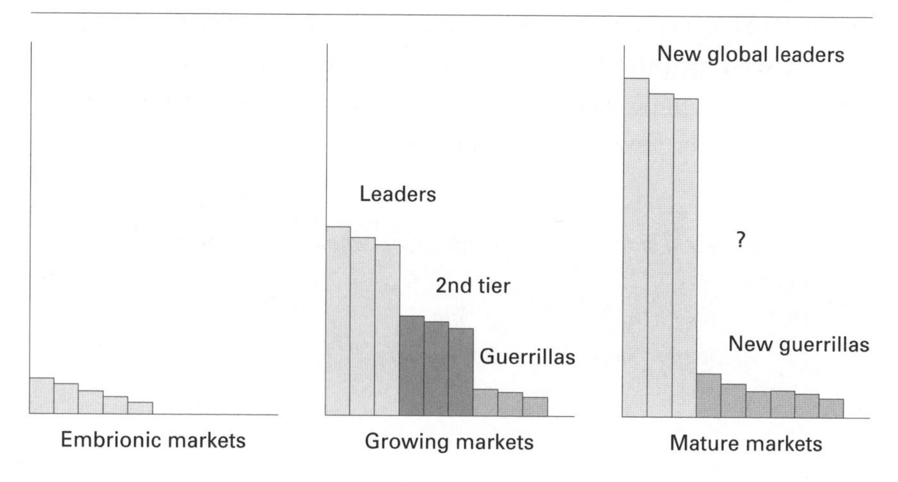

Figure 1.4 illustrates the inexorable movement towards globalization. As markets mature, the big ones get bigger and lots of new, small firms start up to fill the gap by the ones that have disappeared (see the right of Figure 1.4). Those that become 'stuck in the middle' suffer a difficult time, as they cannot compete against the economies of scale and scope of the leaders, and they certainly cannot compete with the low cost base and entrepreneurial speed of the newer small companies.

Globalization provides great opportunities for SMEs.

Today, for example, there are very few car companies in the world and in the UK, about six supermarkets account for almost all grocery spending.

This, of course, represents a wonderful opportunity for SMEs and it is no accident that governments in the West are putting so much resource into encouraging SMEs to grow by exporting.

The final challenge is customer power. With the progress of technology, the days have gone when companies could pump information into the mushy, waiting brains of customers and sit back and wait for a response. Today's customers know far more about suppliers then suppliers know about them and the power lies very much in their hands.

For evidence of this (provided on request), the top ROI companies on the FTSE every year for two decades up to 2000 either went bankrupt or were acquired. The first decade of the 21st century was no better, and as can be seen from the boxed quote relating to the United States, there were many such casualties.

> *There are two sides of the balance sheet – the left side and the right side.*
> *On the left side there is nothing right,*
> *And on the right side, there is nothing left.*

What continuously successful companies do to meet these challenges

Figure 1.5 summarizes decades of scholarly research into what continuously successful organizations do. As can be seen, they have excellent products/services, their managerial processes are up-to-date and efficient, their people enjoy working for the organization and lastly, they all have excellent marketing, which I will go on to explain in the next chapter.

Figure 1.5 How excellent companies succeed continuously

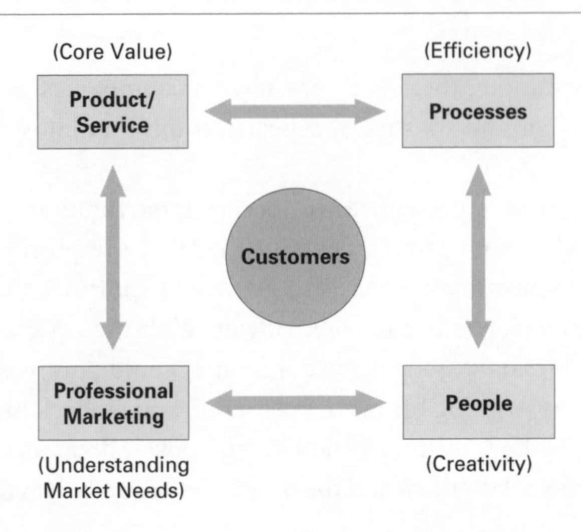

Winning companies have excellent products, efficient processes, happy employees and excellent marketing.

Lest readers should think this looks a little simplistic, the case below summarizes the findings from 137 scholarly articles over a period of 30 years about what are the components of excellent marketing. Please take just a few moments to study this list, because I will go on to explain each in more detail in later chapters, but in a way that will lead to actionable propositions for all SMEs.

Over 40 years of research into the link between long-run financial success and excellent marketing strategies reveal the following:

Excellent Strategies	**Weak Strategies**
• Understand markets in depth.	• Always talk about products.
• Target needs-based segments.	• Target product categories.
• Make a specific offer to each segment.	• Make similar offers to all segments.
• Have clear differentiation, positioning and branding.	• Have no differentiation and poor positioning and branding.
• Leverage their strengths and minimize their weaknesses.	• Have little understanding of their strengths and weaknesses.
• Anticipate the future.	• Plan using historical data.

We can now proceed to a short Chapter 2 to complete our introduction, before setting out in subsequent chapters the actionable propositions, essential to developing a winning strategy for growth in sales and profits.

Actions

NB: After Chapter 4, you will be asked to complete your strategy one section at a time until, by the end of the book, you will have developed a winning strategy to grow your sales and profits. For now, please just make your own notes based on the points I have made in this introductory chapter.

Getting rid of that big managerial nonsense

02

By the end of this chapter, readers will understand:

- The limited value of financial statements such as Profit and Loss Accounts and Balance Sheets
- The reason why forecasts and budgets are in the main ineffective
- What marketing is
- What the components of a Business Plan are and where the Marketing Plan fits in
- What the components are of a winning marketing strategy

Don't get misled by all that financial information

The first crucial point I want to make in this chapter is that most of the financial information is pretty pointless in the absence of market-based information.

Let's start by having a quick look at the financial information in Table 2.1 and Table 2.2. Although based on a real company, rest assured this data is entirely fictitious to illustrate the point I wish to make.

Table 2.1 InterTech's five-year profit performance

Performance (£million)	Base Year	1	2	3	4	5
Sales Revenue	£254	£293	£318	£387	£431	£454
– Cost of goods sold	135	152	167	201	224	236
Gross Contribution	£119	£141	£151	£186	£207	£218
– Manufacturing overhead	48	58	63	82	90	95
– Marketing & Sales	18	23	24	26	27	28
– Research & Development	22	23	23	25	24	24
Net Profit	£16	£22	£26	£37	£50	£55
Return on Sales (%)	6.3%	7.5%	8.2%	9.6%	11.6%	12.1%
Assets	£141	£162	£167	£194	£205	£206
Assets (% of sales)	56%	55%	53%	50%	48%	45%
Return on Assets (%)	11.3%	13.5%	15.6%	19.1%	24.4%	26.7%

Table 2.2 InterTech's five-year market-based performance

Performance (£million)	Base Year	1	2	3	4	5
Market Growth	18.3%	23.4%	17.6%	34.4%	24.0%	17.9%
InterTech Sales Growth (%)	12.8%	17.4%	11.2%	27.1%	16.5%	10.9%
Market Share (%)	20.3%	19.1%	18.4%	17.1%	16.3%	14.9%
Customer Retention (%)	88.2%	87.1%	85.0%	82.2%	80.9%	77.0%
New Customers (%)	11.7%	12.9%	14.9%	24.1%	22.5%	29.2%
% Dissatisfied Customers	13.6%	14.3%	16.1%	17.3%	18.9%	19.6%
Relative Product Quality	+10%	+8%	+5%	+3%	+1%	0%
Relative Service Quality	+0%	+0%	–20%	–3%	–5%	–8%
Relative New Product Sales	+8%	+8%	+7%	+5%	+1%	–4%

Without going into too much detail, the headlines are (approximately):

- a doubling of sales over a five-year period;
- a doubling of gross contribution;
- a doubling of return on sales;
- an increase in asset turnover;
- a tripling of return on assets.

On the face of it, this looks like a brilliant performance, until you look at the market-based information in Table 2.2 over the same five-year period:

- The market grew faster than InterTech every year.
- InterTech's market share dropped from 20.3 per cent to 14.9 per cent.
- They used to keep almost 90 per cent of their customers. Now they are losing over 20 per cent every year.
- Dissatisfied customers (from market research) have risen from 13.6 per cent to 19.6 per cent.
- InterTech used to have a superior product. Now it is the same as their competitors' products.
- Their service quality is negative in the marketplace.
- Their new product sales compared with the market are negative.

The excellent performance of InterTech was only possible in a growth market. It was losing its traction in the market and when the market matured, InterTech went bankrupt.

Even the stats about their lack of customer retention is misleading, because a quick glance at Table 2.3 shows that InterTech's customer retention is best (even though it isn't good) in the worst segment in the market whereas its worst performance is in the best segment (only 11 per cent of all sales, but almost 25 per cent of all industry profits).

Table 2.3 Measurement of customer retention by segment profitability

	Total Market	Segment 1	Segment 2	Segment 3	Segment 4	Segment 5	Segment 6
Percentage of market represented by segment	100.0	14.8	9.5	27.1	18.8	18.8	11.0
Percentage of all profits in total market produced by segment	100.0	7.1	4.9	14.7	21.8	28.5	23.0
Ratio of profit produced by segment to weight of segment in total population	1.00	0.48	0.52	0.54	1.16	1.52	2.09
Defection rate	23%	20%	17%	15%	28%	30%	35%

The whole point of this little case history is that:

- InterTech did well financially in a rapidly growing market.
- Over the five-year period, their market/customer performance was truly appalling.
- Their awful market performance was hidden by the financial reporting.
- Soon after this market matured, InterTech went out of business.

So, financial information tells the directors very little about a firm's underlying performance, especially in growth markets, where Mickey Mouse and Donald Duck ought to be capable of making profits. But since such growth markets are hard to find today, the directors desperately need **market-based** information in order to assess the health and prospects for their organization.

> *Financial information tells directors very little about a firm's underlying performance.*

The second point to make about P&L Accounts is that there is only one line for revenue and lots of other lines for costs. The reason for saying this is that the whole point of this book (that is, how to generate profitable revenue) is not captured in board meetings and typically, the discussion of directors revolves around **costs**.

The third point relates to the pointlessness of Balance Sheets. Just look at Tables 2.4, 2.5 and 2.6.

Table 2.4 Balance Sheet

Assets	Liabilities
Land Buildings Plant Vehicles etc	Shares Loans Overdrafts etc
£100 million	**£100 million**

Table 2.5 Balance Sheet

Assets	Liabilities
Land	Shares
Buildings	Loans
Plant	Overdrafts
Vehicles	etc
etc	
£100 million	**£900 million**

Table 2.6 Balance Sheet

Assets	Liabilities
Land	Shares
Buildings	Loans
Plant	Overdrafts
Vehicles	etc
etc	
Goodwill £800m	
£900 million	**£900 million**

As you know, the purpose of a Balance Sheet is that it should **balance** (that is, the left side – what we own – should match the sources of finance). These are labelled Assets and Liabilities. The problem occurs when a predator offers you £100 million and of course, you refuse and eventually settle for a sale price of £900 million. The problem now, of course, is that the Balance Sheet no longer balances. This doesn't present a problem to accountants, however, as a sneaky little balancing factor is now added, labelled 'goodwill' – in this case £800 million. What this £800 million balancing figure is, of course, is the size of the mistake made by accountants in valuing a company and the first time the size of the mistake comes to light is when someone buys it!

The real value of a company lies in its relationships with its customers via its brands.

Yes, of course I know and understand the international financial rules (having been Chairman of a global brand valuation company), but the point I am making here is that tangible assets in most organizations rarely represent the real value of the company, which resides in brands, relationships with customers and the like, which are not allowed to appear on Balance Sheets.

One of the best examples of this is shown in Table 2.7. Proctor & Gamble (no idiots!) paid £31 billion for Gillette, but got only £4 billion of tangible assets.

Table 2.7 Intangibles

P&G paid £31 billion for Gillette, but bought only £4 billion of tangible assets

Gillette brand	£4.0 billion
Duracell brand	£2.5 billion
Oral B	£2.0 billion
Braun	£1.5 billion
Retail and supplier network	£10.0 billion
Gillette innovative capability	£7.0 billion
Total: £27.0 billion	

SOURCE: David Haigh, Chairman of Brand Finance, *Marketing Magazine*, 1 April 2005

Figure 2.1 Asset breakdown for the top 10 countries by enterprise value (US $ millions, 2015)

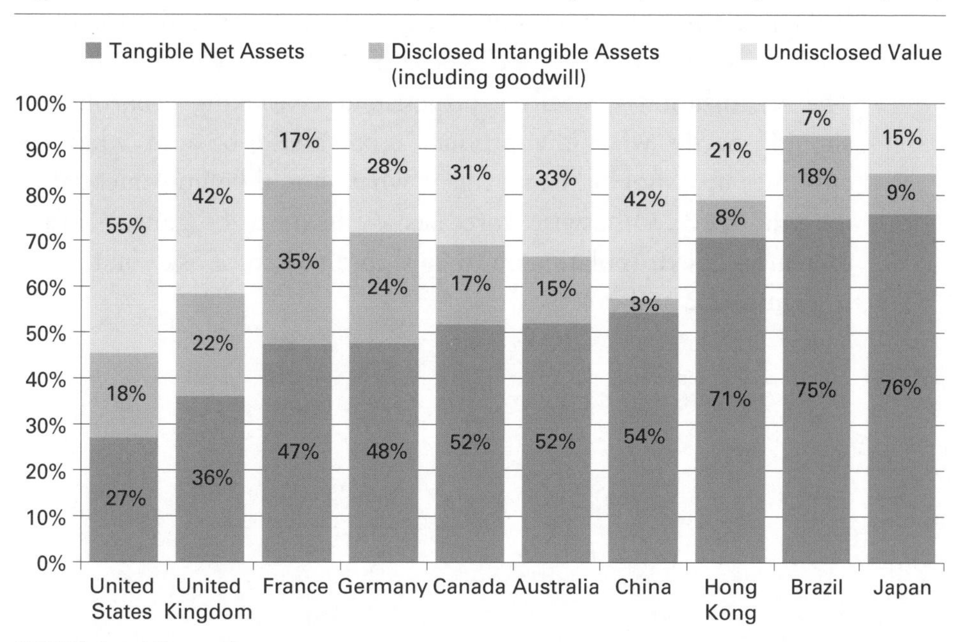

SOURCE: Brand Finance plc

Figure 2.1 shows that in the United States, 73 per cent of all corporate value resides in intangible assets, whilst in the UK it is 64 per cent. Interestingly, the global intangible value of all quoted companies is 53 per cent.

The whole point in providing these figures is to remind smaller companies that their real value resides in their relationship with their markets and their customers, a topic that I will expand on later in this chapter.

The limited value of forecasts and budgets

Most forecasts are merely an extrapolation of a company's own stupidity.

Most forecasts are based on an organization's existing database. Yet a moment's reflection will reveal that this database consists of sales to customers. When I was an inexperienced salesman in London many years ago, I used to sell the products I found easiest to sell to those customers who treated me nicely (those products were frequently the ones on special offer – that is, offered at a discount). If the resulting sales figures are used as the basis of future forecasts, it can be seen that this is a classic case of the tail wagging the dog. The organization – ideally a professional marketing department – should specify what the product mix should be and what the customer mix should be and this is what should be implemented by the sales force. Otherwise, forecasts are likely to be guilty – in the extreme – of extrapolating our own stupidity. Let me ask you to refer to Figures 2.2 and 2.3.

Figure 2.2 Objective based on last year's sales

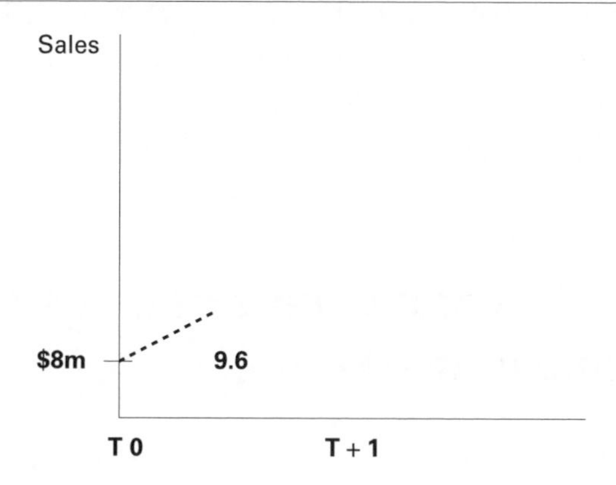

Figure 2.3 Objective based on market positioning

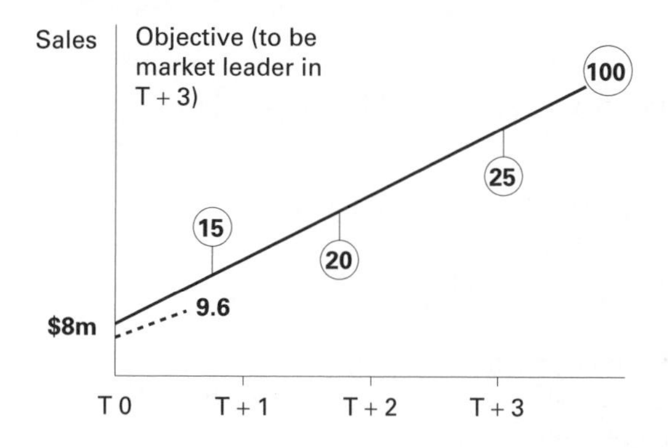

In a traditional (old fashioned) company, given US $8 million of sales last year and with a target (forecast) of +20 per cent next year, the figure that goes into the budget for next year is US $9.6 million. However, had this company done it properly, it might have said: 'Our objective is to be market leader in three years' time. Given a market of US $100 million and market leadership being, say, 25 per cent, it can easily be seen from Figure 2.3 that we should be going for US $15 million next year, *not* US $9.6 million.' Okay, so this is a hypothetical example, but I hope readers will understand the message about forecasting and budgeting.

Of US and European firms 90 per cent think that budgets are cumbersome and unreliable, providing neither predictability nor control. They are backward-looking and inflexible. Instead of focusing managers' time on customers, the real source of income, they focus their attention on satisfying the boss, that is, the budget becomes the purpose. Cheating in all budget regimes is endemic. The result is fear, inefficiency, sub-optimization and waste. In Enron, the pressure was so great, they broke the law and destroyed the enterprise.

What are the components of a business plan and the role of marketing?

> *Any objective must be quantified otherwise it is not an objective.*

Table 2.8 shows what a typical business plan should look like.

Table 2.8 Corporate objectives and strategies

- Corporate Objective (what):
  - Profit
- Corporate Strategies (how):
  - facilities (operations, R&D, IT, distribution, etc)
  - people (personnel)
  - money (finance)
  - products and markets (marketing)
  - other (CSR, image, etc)

This table is most important in the context of this whole book. The first point to notice is that any objective must be quantifiable, otherwise it is not an objective. Hence words like 'maximize', 'minimize', 'penetrate', etc are **not** objectives. Thus, there can only be one corporate objective in business, which is to make a **profit**.

> *Budgets are cumbersome and unreliable, providing neither predictability nor control.*

A strategy in this context is to specify *how* the corporate objective is to be achieved and as can be seen from Table 2.8, these are the following:

- Facilities such as manufacturing, distribution, etc. It would clearly make a major difference to operations if either of these were to be outsourced.
- People, that is, the size and character of the labour force.
- Money, that is, whether to issue shares or to use net free cash flow to fund major projects.
- Products and markets, that is, which products or services to sell into which markets. This I will call 'marketing' for the purpose of this book.
- Other, such as CSR. Here, it should be stressed that in the best companies in the world, CSR is an integral strategy of profit-making.

Now let me focus on the crucial importance of the strategy of products and markets. When I was Marketing Director of Canada Dry, we *always* produced our draft strategic plan first for which products we were going to sell into which markets, to what effect. However, we carefully checked our draft strategies with our manufacturing, distribution and financial colleagues in order to be certain that we were not setting unrealistic objectives. Once these were signed off by our colleagues from other disciplines we would then produce our strategic marketing plan, which became the basis for all the other disciplines to produce their own strategic plans. These were then summarized into a corporate strategic business plan for the next three years.

From this, it will be seen that the basis of *all* corporate activity was the strategic marketing plan. A little thought should be enough to convince any business person that the strategic marketing plan should be completed first (based obviously on our asset base capabilities), so it is to this crucial document that we now turn our attention.

It will also be obvious that the remainder of this book, and the basis of developing a winning strategy, will be devoted to developing a strategic marketing plan.

The strategic plan must always precede the tactical plan.

The components of a winning marketing strategy

Now we have seen the crucial importance of marketing strategy as a driver of corporate strategy, we can look at the components of a strategic marketing plan (see Table 2.9). In subsequent chapters, I will explain in more detail what each component should contain, with templates for readers to put their own date into.

For now, all that is necessary, is to explain why it is a 'strategic' marketing plan and not a 'tactical' marketing plan, which follows the preparation of the strategic marketing plan.

The importance of strategy cannot be over-emphasized.

Table 2.9 The contents of a strategic marketing plan (for three years, fewer than 20 pages)

- Financial summary
- Market overview
  - how the market works
  - key segments and their needs
- SWOT analyses of segments
- Portfolio summary of SWOTS
- Assumptions
- Objectives and strategies
- Budget for three years

The plan for what is to be sold to whom must always come first in business planning.

Figure 2.4 Strategy and tactics matrix

		Strategy	
		Ineffective	Effective
Tactics	Efficient	Die (quickly)	Thrive
	Inefficient	Die (slowly)	Survive

Firstly, let's settle for some simple definitions. 'Strategy' means doing the right things. 'Tactics' means doing things right.

Now look at the top-left box in Figure 2.4. What it says is that implementing the wrong strategy efficiently is likely to lead to a quick death! If you have any doubt about this, now look at the analogy of a salesperson shown in Figure 2.5.

Figure 2.5 The salesperson analogy

	A Salesperson	
	Clever	Stupid
Lazy	✓✓✓	✓
Hard-working	✓✓✓ ✓✓✓	✗

Doing the wrong thing efficiently will lead to an early death.

In particular, look at the bottom right-hand box. Clearly, making a stupid salesperson work hard is likely to offend twice as many customers and double the chaos!

Hence my assertion concerning Figure 2.4 that doing the wrong thing well isn't the most productive way forward.

So, I hope I have convinced you that developing a strategy before you begin to think about tactics is the most effective way of continuous growth in your sales and profits.

Most of the basics have now been covered, so we can now move to a brief section on what marketing is and why it is the cornerstone of all successful organizations.

What marketing is and its role in continuous organizational success

Marketing is a process for identifying and creating sustainable competitive advantage. The important words here are 'sustainable competitive advantage'. Competitive advantage can be achieved in many ways, such as through a technological breakthrough (but today such breakthroughs are easily copied), cost reductions, (but these are rarely sustainable), sponsorship and the like.

Sustainable competitive advantage results from embedded relationships with customers through value propositions that deliver superior value to customers, the only real source of long-term super profits.

This is what this book is about.

The purpose of strategic marketing is to create sustainable competitive advantage.

Finally, in this chapter, let us make it clear what we mean by the term 'marketing'. The overall purpose of strategic marketing and its principal focus is the identification and creation of sustainable competitive advantage.

Marketing is a process for:

- defining markets in terms of needs;
- quantifying the needs of the customer groups (segments) within these markets;
- developing value propositions to meet these needs;

- communicating these value propositions to all those in the organization responsible for delivering them and getting their buy-in to their role-playing, an appropriate part in delivering the value propositions (usually only communications);
- measuring the value actually delivered.

For this process to be effective, organizations need to be customer-driven. Figure 2.6 summarizes this.

Marketing concerns what is sold and to whom and why customers should buy from us.

Please note that it is the first two boxes ('Define markets & understand value', and 'Develop value propositions') that will form the core of this book, as they are the principal components of a winning marketing strategy.

We will only briefly touch on boxes three and four, as they represent the first-year implementation and measurement of the strategic marketing plan. We will use this figure (map of marketing) as the basics of all the remaining chapters of this book.

One last point remains to be made about the above definition of marketing and this relates to the measurement of sustainable competitive advantage.

Figure 2.6 Map of the marketing domain

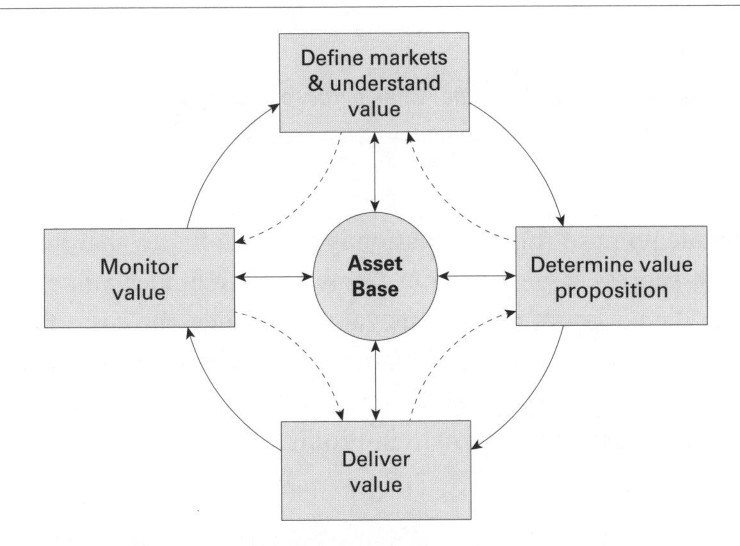

Figure 2.7 is a simplified version of how stock exchanges all over the world work.

'Return', (the vertical axis), represents the declared financial results of organizations. 'Risk' (the horizontal axis), represents the investment communities' assessment of the likelihood that the profit forecasts of organizations will happen. The red line (the Beta) represents the average of both axes, so, for example, the point on the Beta of ② (risk and return) is the weighted average return on investment of all organizations in a particular sector. This is known as the 'Cost of Capital'. For the purpose of this explanation, let us assume that the cost of capital in a particular sector is 10 per cent. So, any organization earning 11 per cent or more is creating shareholder value, whilst any organization earning less than 10 per cent is destroying shareholder value.

Figure 2.7 Financial risk and return

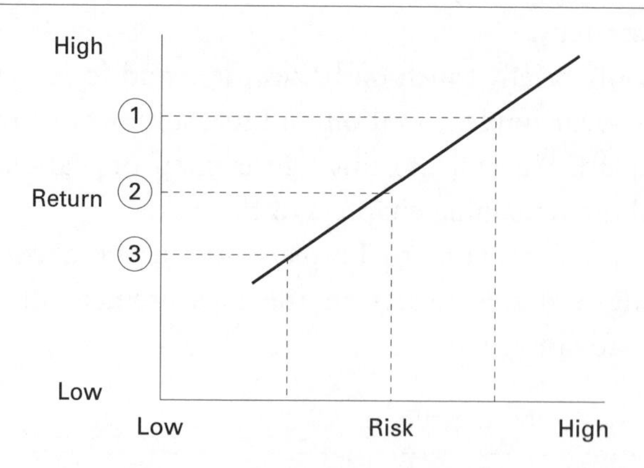

> *Shareholder value added is the whole purpose of business, otherwise you should put your money in the bank.*

The whole point of this explanation is twofold: firstly, that in capital markets, success is measured in terms of shareholder value added, having taken account of the time value of money, the cost of capital and the perceived risks of the declared commercial strategies; secondly, investors aren't fooled by short-term boosts in profit and are only interested in **sustainable** growth in profits.

The answer should be fairly obvious. Take, for example, an SME with £20,000 invested at a cost of capital of 10 per cent. Making a net profit of £1,500 means that £500 of shareholder value has been destroyed. A profit of £2,500 means that £500 of shareholder value has been created. It would indeed be a strange kind of SME that settled for destroying shareholder value.

The remainder of this book contains actionable propositions for growing shareholder value.

Actions

I repeat here what I said at the end of Chapter 1. Please make your own notes based on the points I have made here.

Understand the real meaning of customer value 03

At the end of this chapter you will:

- Understand what a value proposition is
- Know how to quantify your value propositions
- Understand the crucial importance of the name – the brand – you give to your value propositions

Introduction

Before moving to the real action, there follows a chapter on value propositions and branding, as to understand these essential prerequisites of successful strategy-making will help to make the resulting plans much more powerful.

What is value?

The very word 'value' is highly contentious, because it totally depends on whose point of view is being taken and the context in which the word is used.

Before I give you my own interpretation of the term, (which will be used throughout the remainder of this book), let me share with you some common usage of the term. I will do this as briefly as possible and only in the interest of not wishing to be labelled a biased consultant.

Value chain analysis

It is important to understand the meaning of 'value'.

Firstly, there is Michael Porter's well-known concept of value chain analysis in *Competitive Strategy* (The Free Press, 1980). Porter's concept of value added is an incremental one; he focuses on how successive activities change the value of goods and services as they pass through various stages of a value chain. The analysis disaggregates a firm into its major activities in order to understand the behaviour of costs and the existing and potential sources of differentiation. It determines how the firm's own value chain interacts with the value chains of suppliers, customers and competitors. Companies gain competitive advantage by performing some or all of these activities at lower cost or with greater differentiation than their competitors.

Shareholder value analysis (SVA)

Secondly, there is Alfred Rappaport's equally well-known research on shareholder value analysis, *Creating Shareholder Value* (The Free Press, 1986). Rappaport's concept of value added focuses less on processes than Porter, and acts more as a final gateway in decision-making, although it can be used at multiple levels within a firm. It is the process of analysing how decisions affect the net present value of cash to shareholders. The analysis measures a company's ability to earn more than its total cost of capital. Within business units, SVA measures the value the unit has created by analysing cash flows over time. At the corporate level, SVA provides a framework for evaluating options for improving shareholder value by determining the trade-offs between reinvesting in existing businesses, investing in new businesses and returning cash to stockholders. This was touched on in the opening chapter.

Customer value

A third way of looking at value added is the customer's perception of value. Unfortunately, despite exhaustive research by academics and practitioners around the world, this elusive concept has proved almost impossible to pin down: what constitutes [customer] value – even in a single product category – appears to be highly personal and idiosyncratic. Nevertheless, the individual customer's perception of the extra value represented by different products and services cannot be easily dismissed: in the guise of measures such as customer satisfaction and customer loyalty it is known to be the essence of brand success, and the whole basis of the new science of relationship marketing.

Accounting value

Finally, there is the accountant's definition of value added:

Value added = sales revenue – purchases and services

Effectively, this is a snapshot picture from the annual accounts of how the revenue from a sales period has been distributed, and how much is left over for reinvestment after meeting all costs, including shareholder dividends. Although this figure will say something about the past viability of a business, in itself it does not provide a guide to future prospects.

One reason that the term 'value added' has come to be used rather carelessly is that all these concepts of value, although different, are not mutually exclusive. Porter's value chain analysis is one of several extremely useful techniques for identifying potential new competitive market strategies. Rappaport's SVA approach can be seen as a powerful tool that enables managers to cost out the long-term financial implications of pursuing one or other of the competitive strategies that have been identified. Customer perceptions are clearly a major driver (or destroyer) of annual audited accounting value in all companies, whatever strategy is pursued.

Accounting value only represents what has been achieved in the past.

However, most companies today accept that value added, as defined by their annual accounts, is really only a record of what they achieved in the past, and that financial targets in themselves are insufficient as business objectives. Many companies are now convinced that focusing on more intangible measures of value added such as brand equity, customer loyalty, or customer satisfaction are the new route to achieving financial results.

Common sense (and with apologies for this quasi-academic discussion), might argue that developing strong product or service offerings, and building up a loyal, satisfied customer base will usually require a series of one- to two-year investment plans in any business. Also, such is the universal distrust of marketing strategies and forecasts, it is common practice in most companies to write off marketing as a cost within each year's budget. It is rare for such expenditure to be treated as an investment that will deliver results over a number of years, but research shows that companies that are able to do this create a lasting competitive edge.

So, I will quantify what a value proposition is from the customer's perspectives.

Differentiation

For any organization today, creating differentiation that the customer needs is more challenging than at any time in history, but it remains at the heart of successful marketing. More importantly, it remains the key to a company's survival.

Differentiation that is wanted by customers is the key to commercial success.

The truth is that if you are in an overcrowded market where you don't stand out, all lowering prices will achieve is to erode your margins and, unless your business costs are lower than anyone else's, discounting is a losing game.

The alternative, of course, is successful differentiation. If you can't come up with something genuinely different and better, there isn't much future for your company.

However, before I explain how to go about this, I want to point out that because of technological advances, product differentiation is unlikely to win in the long run, because this is comparatively easy to emulate today.

Much more likely, differentiation will result from the way you relate to your customers.

CASE STUDY Excellence is not enough – differentiation is essential

One of the big carmakers organized a competitor comparison day, buying one example of every rival model in a particular category and lining them up in a row. Each car was silver and the badges had been removed. Not only could the assembled experts not tell them apart, they couldn't even pick out their own car.

The message? All were excellent, but striving in the same direction as everyone else is an exhausting treadmill that offers only temporary advantage. So, be excellent, but above all, be different.

Source: Alistair Dryburgh, 'Everything you know about business is wrong', *Management Today*, October 2014, p15

For now, let's call this 'customer service' and I will explain later in this book the myriad of forms that customer service can take. One such form is the result of market segmentation and I devote a whole chapter to this fundamental form of differentiation and competitive advantage.

For now, however, all I want you to understand is that differentiation is the key to commercial success and must be encapsulated somehow in a value proposition. Let's start by looking at Figure 3.1 on strategic purchasing.

Figure 3.1 Strategic purchasing

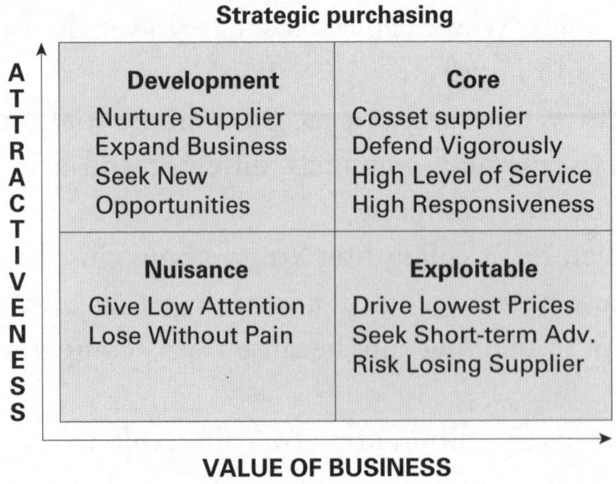

Strategic purchasing

ATTRACTIVENESS

Development Nurture Supplier Expand Business Seek New Opportunities	**Core** Cosset supplier Defend Vigorously High Level of Service High Responsiveness
Nuisance Give Low Attention Lose Without Pain	**Exploitable** Drive Lowest Prices Seek Short-term Adv. Risk Losing Supplier

VALUE OF BUSINESS

Based on: Kraljic, P *HBR* 1 Sept 1983

It is used by most buyers in most markets, the only difference being that the vertical axis is sometimes labelled 'differentiation' (high or low). The most important box to look at is the bottom-right box. Here, the buyer orders a lot and can get it from virtually any supplier, so not surprisingly, buys on price.

The bottom-left box, (low differentiation and the buyer does not purchase a lot), represents a great opportunity for SMEs to take responsibility from the customer by means of outsourcing.

The top-left box, providing an SME offers something different that the customer really values, is an even better opportunity, because even though the customer doesn't buy much, price is rarely important.

By far the best box to occupy is the top-right one. Buyers order a lot and they really value the differentiation offered. Here, it is not unusual for them to pay up to 20 per cent premium to deal with such suppliers.

Buyers will pay a premium price (and buy a lot) for something which is different and which will help them.

The bad news, however, is that the low differentiation axis nearly always leads to very low prices and margins for suppliers. This is all right, however, providing at least some of the main products or services you supply are differentiated and it is to this that we now turn our attention in the context of value propositions.

Start by having a look at your own website. Typically, suppliers' websites say things like:

- We are innovative.
- We have better quality.
- We have a great reputation.
- You can trust us.
- We are the leading provider of...
- We get good results for our customers.
- We are very responsive.
- Blah, Blah, Blah...

Everybody sounds the same and in the main, customers just don't care. Take a look at Figure 3.2 and I defy you to see any difference in what these suppliers claim to be offering.

Figure 3.2 Examples of lack of differentiation

The technology solutions space is crowded and competitive, and it can be difficult to tell the players by their messaging

Competitor 1 '(ABC offers) comprehensive IT services integrated with business insight to reduce costs, improve productivity and assert competitive Advantage.'	**Competitor 2** 'DEF is the No. 1 provider of integrated business, technology, & process solutions on a global delivery platform.'	**Competitor 3** 'GHI provides a broad portfolio of business & technology solutions to help its clients worldwide improve their business performance. Our core portfolio comprises information technology, applications, & business process services, as well as information technology transformation services.'
Competitor 4 'JKL provides consulting and IT services to clients globally – as partners to conceptualise and realise technology driven business transformation initiatives.'	**Competitor 5** 'MNO is the world-leading Information technology consulting, services, and business process out-sourcing organisation that envisioned and pioneered the adoption of the flexible global business practices that today enable companies to operate more efficiently and produce more value.'	**Competitor 6** 'PQR is global management consulting, technology services, & outsourcing company. Committed to delivering innovation, PQR collaborates with its clients to help them become high-performance businesses and governments.'

SOURCE: Malcolm Frank, Senior Vice President, Strategy & Marketing, Cognizant, as presented at ITSMA's Marketing Leadership Forum, April 2006

My definition of a value proposition is 'relative value equals perceived benefits minus costs, which must be positive'.

The Investopedia 2016 definition of a value proposition is: 'A business or marketing statement that summarizes why a consumer should buy a product or use a service. This statement should convince a potential consumer that one product or service will add more value or better solve a problem than other similar offerings'. (See www.investopedia.com/terms/v/valueproposition.asp)

McKinsey's definition (by Lanning and Michaels in June 2000) is: 'A clear, simple statement of the benefits – both tangible and intangible – that the company will provide along with the approximate price it will charge each customer segment for those benefits'. (See www.mckinsey.com/insights/strategy/delivering_value_to_customers)

My own definition is: 'Relative value = perceived benefits minus costs'.

A value proposition should be:

- Distinctive. It must be superior to competitors'.
- Measurable. All value propositions should be based on tangible points of difference that can be quantified in monetary terms.
- Sustainable. It must have a significant life.

Customers expect their business to be better off as a result of dealing with you and you must be able to prove that dealing with you will create advantage for the customer, not merely help them to avoid disadvantage. This is summarized in Figure 3.3 below and please note the key phrase: 'creating advantage, not just avoiding disadvantage'.

Figure 3.3 Creating advantage and avoiding disadvantage

	STRATEGIC	HIGH POTENTIAL
CREATING ADVANTAGE		
AVOIDING DISADVANTAGE		
	KEY OPERATIONAL	SUPPORT

Key: **Strategic** = Issues that will ensure the customer's long-term success.
High potential = Issues that, whilst not crucial currently, could potentially lead to differential advantage for the customer.
Key operational = Issues that, unless solved reasonably quickly, could lead to disadvantage for the customer.
Support = Issues that, whilst of a non-urgent nature such as information availability, nonetheless need to be solved to avoid disadvantage for the customer.

A value proposition has four potential parts, as follows:

- added value (eg revenue gains, improved productivity, service enhancement, speed, etc);
- cost reduction;
- cost avoidance;
- emotional contribution (eg trust, 'feel-good factor', confidence, self-esteem, risk reduction, etc).

The first three are comparatively easy to quantify, the last one less so, although particularly with well-known brands such as SKF, IBM, GE, 3M and the like, they are often high on the business agenda.

An excellent example of this is SKF, the Swedish bearing company. They have a global President of Value Propositions. They tailor them to each customer, but Figure 3.4 below shows a generic value proposition (reproduced with the kind permission of SKF).

Figure 3.4 SKF Quantified Value Proposition

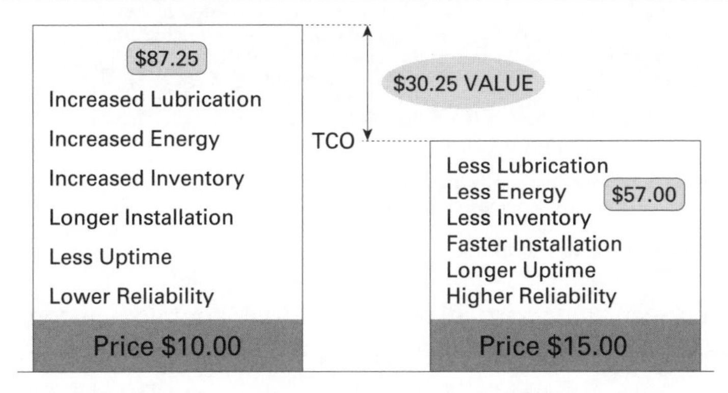

SOURCE: Reproduced with kind permission of SKF, who presented the diagram at Cranfield University's KAM Best Practice Research Club in January 2015

From this it can be seen that over the life of the bearings, the significant premium over the bearings of competitors saves the customer $30.25, representing the quantified added value.

This, of course, is a simple example and value propositions can be more complex. Look, for example, at Michael Porter's well-known value chain, shown in Figure 3.5.

Figure 3.5 Porter's Value Chain (1980)

Support Activities	
Infrastructure	- Legal, Accounting, Financial Management
Human Resource Management	- Personnel, Pay, Recruitment, Training, Manpower Planning, etc
Product & Technology Development	- Product and Process Design, Production Engineering, Market Testing, R&D, etc
Procurement	- Supplier Management, Funding, Subcontracting, Specification

INBOUND LOGISTICS	OPERATIONS	OUTBOUND LOGISTICS	SALES & MARKETING	SERVICING
eg Quality Control Receiving Raw Material Control etc	eg Manufacturing Packaging Production Control Quality Control Maintenance etc	eg Finishing Goods Order Handling Despatch Delivery Invoicing etc	eg Account mgmt Order Taking Promotion Sales Analysis Market Research etc	eg Warranty Maintenance Education / Training Upgrade etc

Value Added - Cost = Profit

Primary Activities

Many activities cross the boundaries - especially information based activities such as: Sales Forecasting, Capacity Planning, Resource Scheduling, Pricing, etc

SOURCE: Porter ME (1980) *Competitive Strategy*, The Free Press: New York

It will be seen that, particularly for a large, complex customer, the opportunities to add value, reduce or avoid costs, are substantial. But this will require the supplier to spend time understanding the intricacies of how the customer's business works from end to end.

> *In B2B markets it is essential to spend time understanding the intricacies of the customer's processes in order to find ways of adding value.*

Figures 3.6 and 3.7 below give some examples of how this is possible, whilst Figure 3.8 gives a real example from Tetra Pak (reproduced from their Cranfield University talks with their kind permission).

Figure 3.6 Sources of differentiation in the value chain

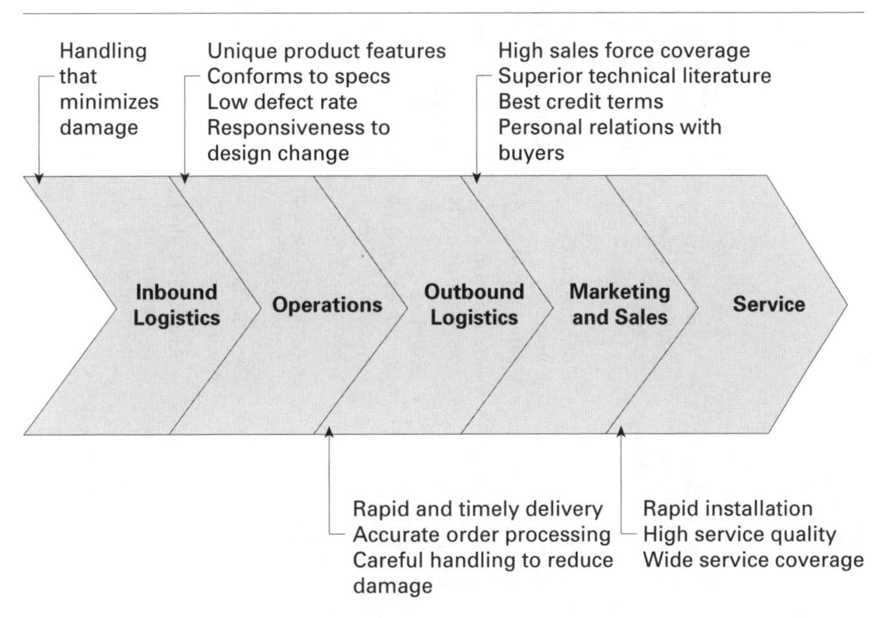

SOURCE: Reproduced with the kind permission of Tetra Pak, presented at Cranfield University

Figure 3.7 How do you add value through key support activities?

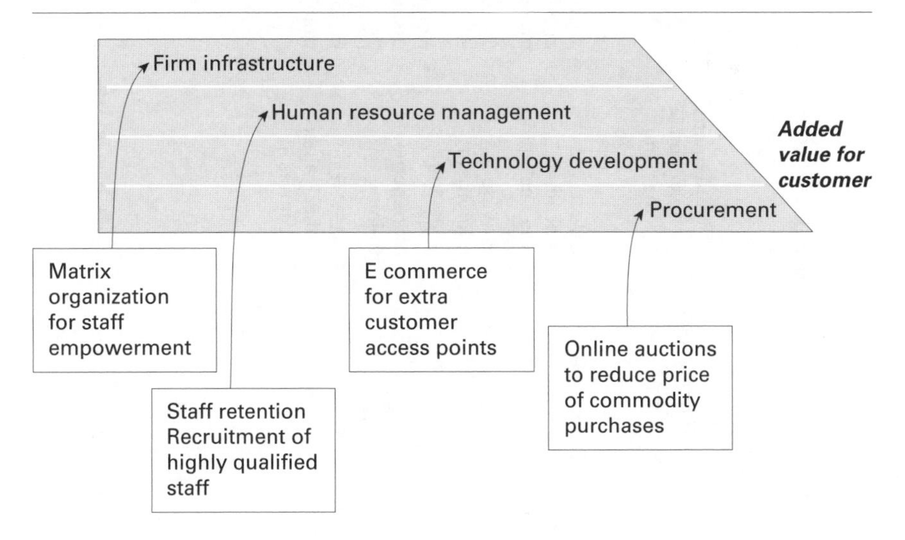

Figure 3.8 Tetra Pak is a multi-stage, multi-level partner

Channel selection	Supply chain analysis	Equipment selection & financing	Installation & start-up	Operational fine-tuning & process flow	Equipment maintenance and parts	Wholesale and retail distribution process flow
• Determine food packaging and performance objectives: – Product quality – Litres of output per hour – Sustainability targets	• Determine distribution requirements: – Shipping frequency and method – Wholesale and retail shelf space – Weight constraints	• Select machinery and packaging • Provide equipment financing • Management training – 15 "Train the Trainer" centres	• Test machinery and factory process flow • Quality testing with distributors • Hone product quality • On-site ops. and maintenance training	• Increase employee productivity and maximize availability of equipment – Human error accounts for most equipment failure	• Optimize parts inventory management – 4 distribution centres for parts • Optimize QC: Who does what to what equipment, when and how – Access to 65 tech service centres • Periodic factory review – Avoid "if it ain't broke, don't fix it"mentality	• Periodically obtain feedback – Wholesaler and retailers • Incorporate feedback into next iteration design

SOURCE: Reproduced with kind permission of Tetra Pak, presented at the Cranfield University KAM Research Club, May 2014

Although Tetra Pak is a large organization, it nonetheless is involved with a technology that hundreds of competitors also understand. The difference is that customers value Tetra Pak more highly because of their attention to detail throughout the value chain.

CASE STUDY

This is an example of a small label company reacting to food manufacturers taking responsibility for almost eliminating their stockholding.

They quantified all of the following:

- It reduces your inventory from six to two weeks.
- It reduces the cash tied up in inventory.
- It reduces the problems when you have a stock-out.
- It reduces stock-out costs (downtime, expedited shipping, overtime).
- It reduces inventory-carrying costs.
- It reduces inventory obsolescence.
- It increases sales when you can make quick changes.
- It eliminates the need to place orders.

And all at the same price.

What are the advantages to the label company?

- They answer the question: 'Why should I buy from you?'.
- They are different from their competitors.
- They reduce the risk of losing a customer to a competitor offering a price reduction.
- They make it more difficult for a customer to leave.
- They become better at the production and distribution processes.
- They can then gain new customers.
- Their sales and profits increase.

In conclusion, I hope I have convinced you that differentiation and quantifiable value propositions are crucial to profitable growth. But before proceeding to spell out in later chapters the kind of analysis that will make this task easier (that is, market segmentation and customer needs analysis), I would like to conclude with a brief section on branding.

Branding

Everything an organization does, from R&D through to after-sales service, manifests itself in the value proposition offered to the customer and, of course, this value proposition has a name on it – either a brand name or the name of the supplying company.

We have already seen in Chapter 1 that it is relationships with market and customers that create wealth for suppliers.

Successful brands:

- build trust;
- have a price/quality trade-off – win/win;
- offer consistently superior value.

The result is super profits through higher volumes and margins.

Unsuccessful brands:

- cut corners;
- reduce costs;
- tell lies;
- add some 'gold' to the packaging;
- etc.

The result is that they eventually become commodities and trade on price.

Although the example given in Figure 3.9 is for a large company, it nonetheless represents all the benefits of powerful value propositions represented by powerful brands.

Everything an organization does is represented by the offer, which has a name attached to it – a brand.

As a key example, brands affect business value by influencing the behaviour of a wide range of Shell's stakeholders, some of which directly impact Shell's P&L (and hence value). Figure 3.9 helps to portray this.

Figure 3.9 Brands increasingly drive business results

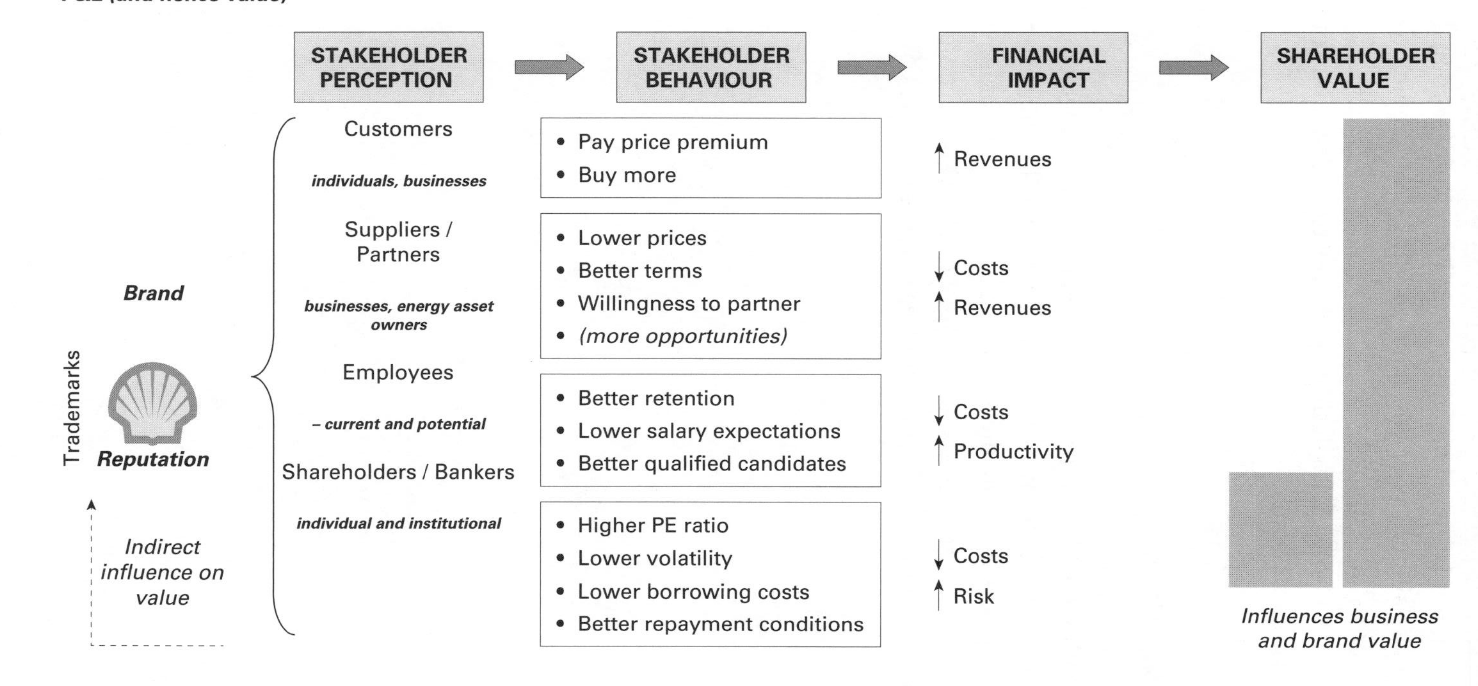

In conclusion and bearing mind that this is not a book on branding, the point I am making is that your brand and/or company name is the most valuable asset you have and this is only going to be as good as your value propositions.

In Chapter 5, I will show you how to understand your markets and customers better.

Actions

Although I haven't yet shown you how to understand your markets and your customers better prior to developing differentiated value propositions, nonetheless, you can have a preliminary attempt here at putting together value propositions. Make a note of your initial efforts and check them out after reading Chapters 5 and 6.

A very practical way to begin planning a profitable future 04

At the end of this chapter readers will know:

- Where to start the process of business planning
- How to develop an outline plan of action

Where to begin?

The first thing that must be understood about business planning is the need to have very clear goals, or objectives. Leaving aside the possibility of a career for members of the family, most SMEs that I am familiar with want the shareholders to get rich either by creating shareholder value added, or by selling the company for a capital sum at some time in the future. For example, I am Chairman of an SME that currently has a turnover of £5 million and we know that it will become a saleable proposition when this reaches £10 million.

The first point to make, then, is that an SME has to set an objective in terms of turnover for a period of at least three years ahead. Let us call this a 'MUST' objective. Later in this chapter I will provide detailed templates for the process I am about to describe here.

Let us look, then, at Figure 4.1.

Figure 4.1 Revenue and profit objectives

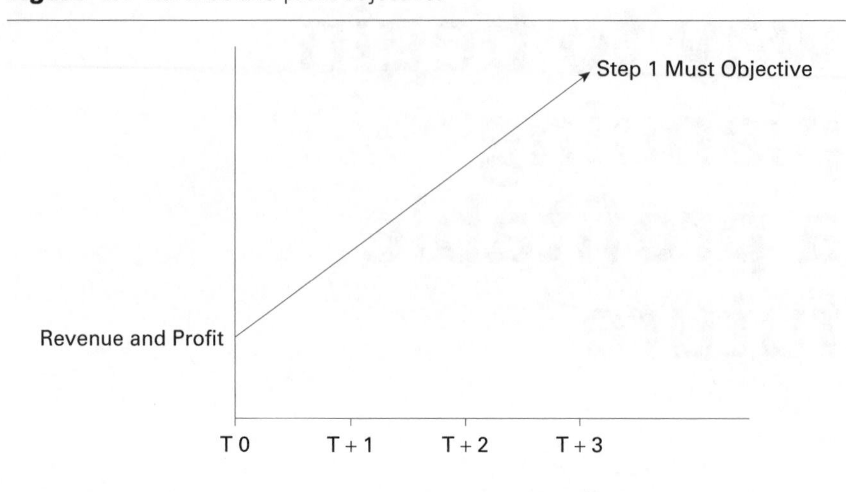

It is crucial to be clear about what your MUST revenue and profit objectives are three years from now.

It will be seen that along the horizontal axis, there is a three-year timescale; on the vertical axis, there is 'Revenue' and 'Profit'. For now, we will concentrate on the 'Revenue' line.

The very first action is to take the Revenue line and project it three years out to reflect your MUST objective. This MUST objective should be the revenue target that has to be achieved for you to achieve your ambitions.

The second task is to project the Revenue line three years out assuming nothing changes. Let's call this the **trend** or **forecast** (see Figure 4.2). The purpose of this is to show you the size of the problem you face (the gap).

Figure 4.2 Forecast assuming no change

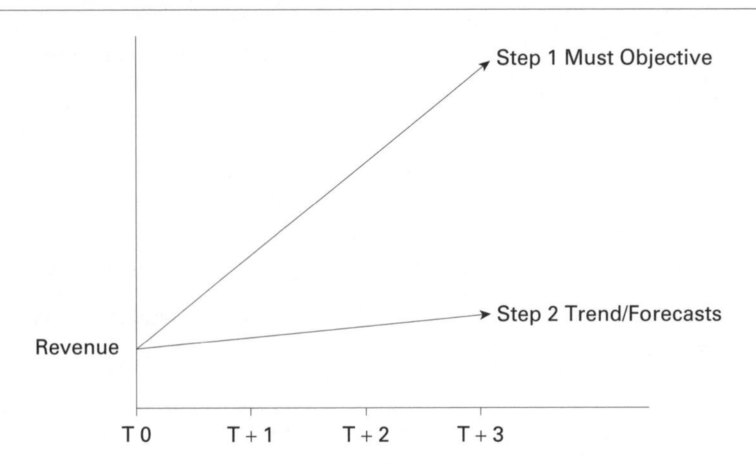

The next thing to do is to calculate how this gap might be filled.

The first action is to consider **productivity** issues. For example, calculate how much extra revenue you could get from the following:

- better product mix;
- better customer mix;
- more sales calls;
- better sales calls;
- increase in prices;
- reduction in discounts;
- charge for deliveries;
- reduction in debtor days;
- etc.

The approximate total from all these should be added to the gap analysis diagram (see Figure 4.3).

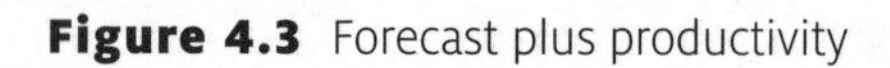

Figure 4.3 Forecast plus productivity

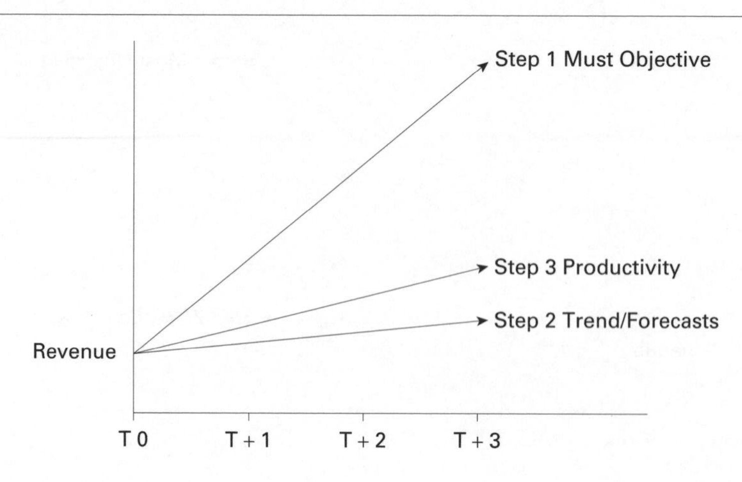

If the gap still hasn't been filled – which is most likely – continue to the next stage.

Product-market table

List your principal products/services and the principal markets into which you sell them, using Table 4.1.

1 Select a business unit, or part of the business, for which you wish to develop a partial plan. Business unit: ____________________

2 Along the top of the table, list the principal products, product groups or services sold by the business unit, ignoring unimportant ones.

Table 4.1 Product–market table

Products: Markets:	1:	2:	3:	4:	5:	6:	7:
1:							
2:							
3:							
4:							
5:							
6:							
7:							

3 Down the left of the table, list the principal markets, or market segments, you sell into, ignoring unimportant ones.

4 Enter your current sales revenue in each box.

Now select only the main boxes. You will soon find out that about 20 per cent of your products/services for markets accounts for about 80 per cent of your revenue.

Concentrate on these. Now, in these main boxes, calculate approximately how much additional revenue you think you can achieve from:

Growth in the market
Growth in your market share } We will label this 'market penetration'

Put the total of the above revenue into the diagram (Figure 4.4).

Figure 4.4 Forecast plus market penetration

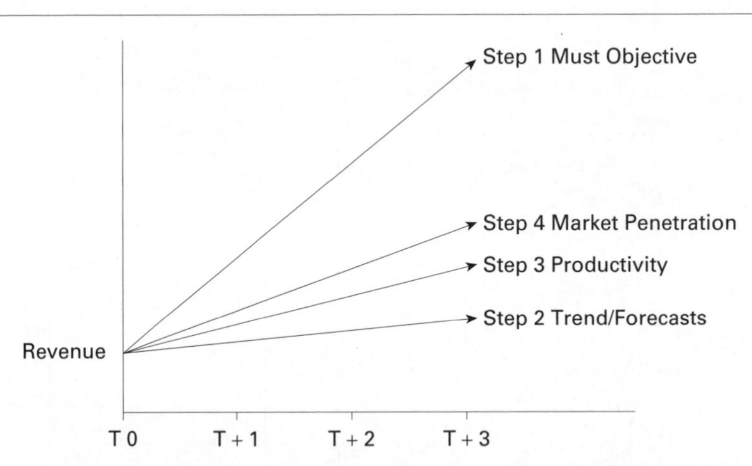

Normally only 20 per cent of your products for markets accounts for 80 per cent of your revenue and profits. Concentrate on these.

If there is still a gap between where you need to be and where your efforts so far will take you, you now need to think about **new products**. So, list the revenue you think you might get from any new product you have in mind and put the total in Figure 4.5.

Figure 4.5 Forecast plus new products

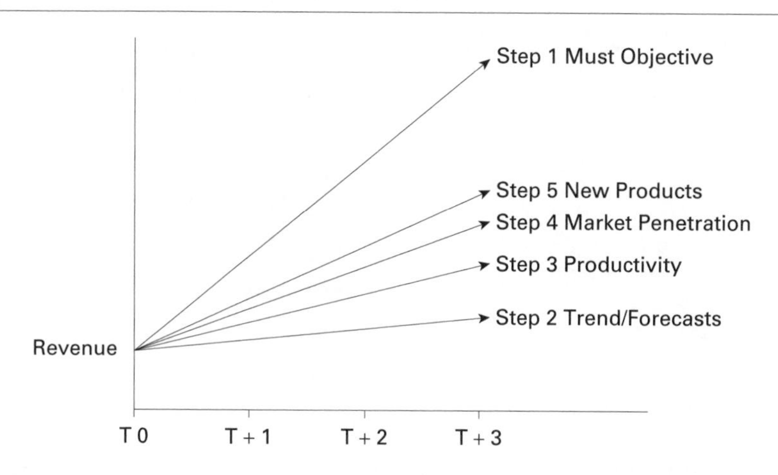

Next, (assuming you still have not reached your MUST objective, list any **new markets** you may be thinking of entering. These could be new vertical markets, or **new countries**. For example, if you sell software to the hotel industry, you might consider entering the retail market or instead of limiting your trading to the UK, you may consider entering France. Estimate the revenue from this over the three-year period and enter the total in Figure 4.6.

Figure 4.6 Forecast plus new markets

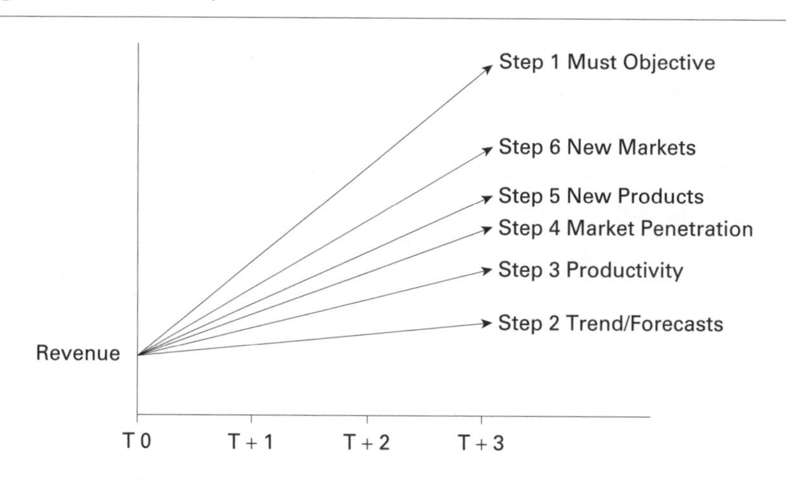

On the assumption that you still haven't achieved your target, now list estimated revenue from the following:

New products/services in new markets.

Enter the resulting revenue in Figure 4.7.

Figure 4.7 Forecast plus new products in new markets

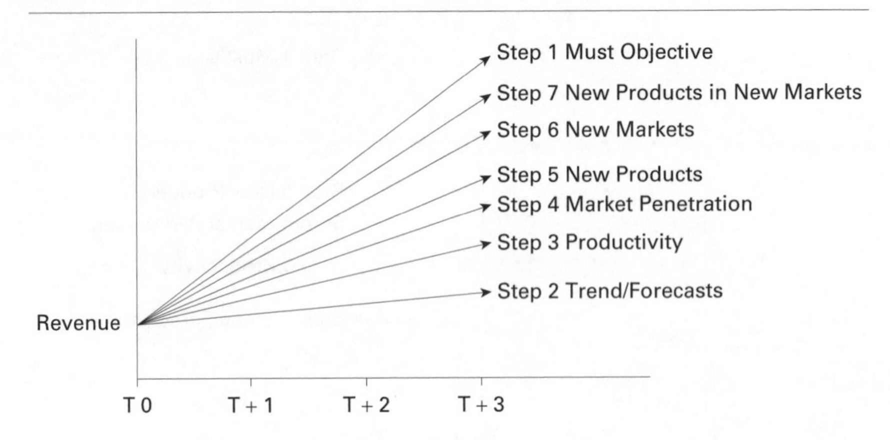

If, as is possible, you still haven't achieved your MUST revenue objective, you have exhausted every 'lever' managers can pull to achieve their objective. At least, however, you have now quantified the gap you still have to fill.

This gap can only be filled by the following:

- acquisitions;
- joint ventures;
- licensing;
- etc.

A quick look at Figure 4.8 will indicate the process you have just been through. Whilst not wishing to sound 'academic', I want to stress that most of our very best managerial tools and techniques have been initiated by scholars studying best practice and turning their findings into processes.

Figure 4.8 Ansoff Matrix

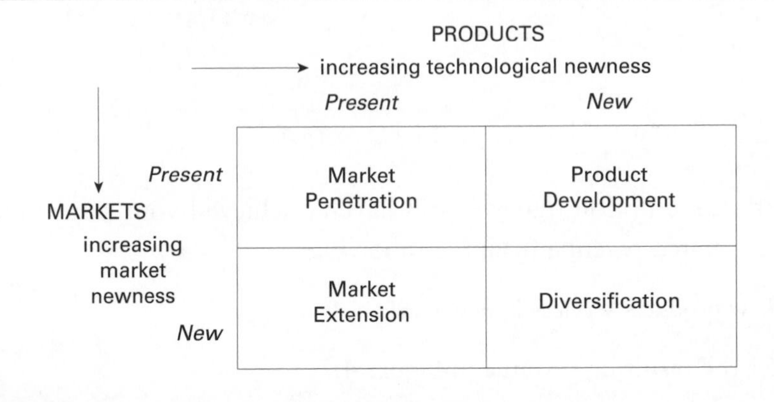

From this, it can be seen that the exercise you have just completed is represented by each of the four boxes in the Ansoff Matrix.

The top-left box is where you are at present. This is where all your expertise resides – with your present products sold to your present markets/customers. Improving your productivity here and looking for market growth and/or market share growth is obviously the least risky business strategy to employ.

If you cannot get the growth you need from this first box, the next least risky box is to introduce new products/services to your existing markets/customer, because your existing customers know and trust you.

The bottom-left box is very risky, because you are entering new markets where both you and your brand are unknown. Consider Walmart's disaster in the German market and Tesco's in the American market. Both assumed that their successful trading model would work abroad. But this is rarely the case.

Clearly, the riskiest strategy of all is the bottom-right box, new products/services in new markets.

So each of the boxes in the Ansoff Matrix represent vectors of risk, with the result that the further you travel from top-left to bottom-right, so the level of risk rises.

In reality, there are not only four boxes in the Ansoff Matrix, because there are degrees of new product development; these range from adding the 'miracle ingredient x' to something new to the world, as well as degrees of new market extension from entering an adjacent market to entering a totally different market.

Concentrate your best efforts on your current products and markets.

Figure 4.9 summarizes in a more sophisticated way the process you have just been through. Careful examination will reveal that it encapsulates every possible strategy that any organization could embrace.

Figure 4.9 Types of objective

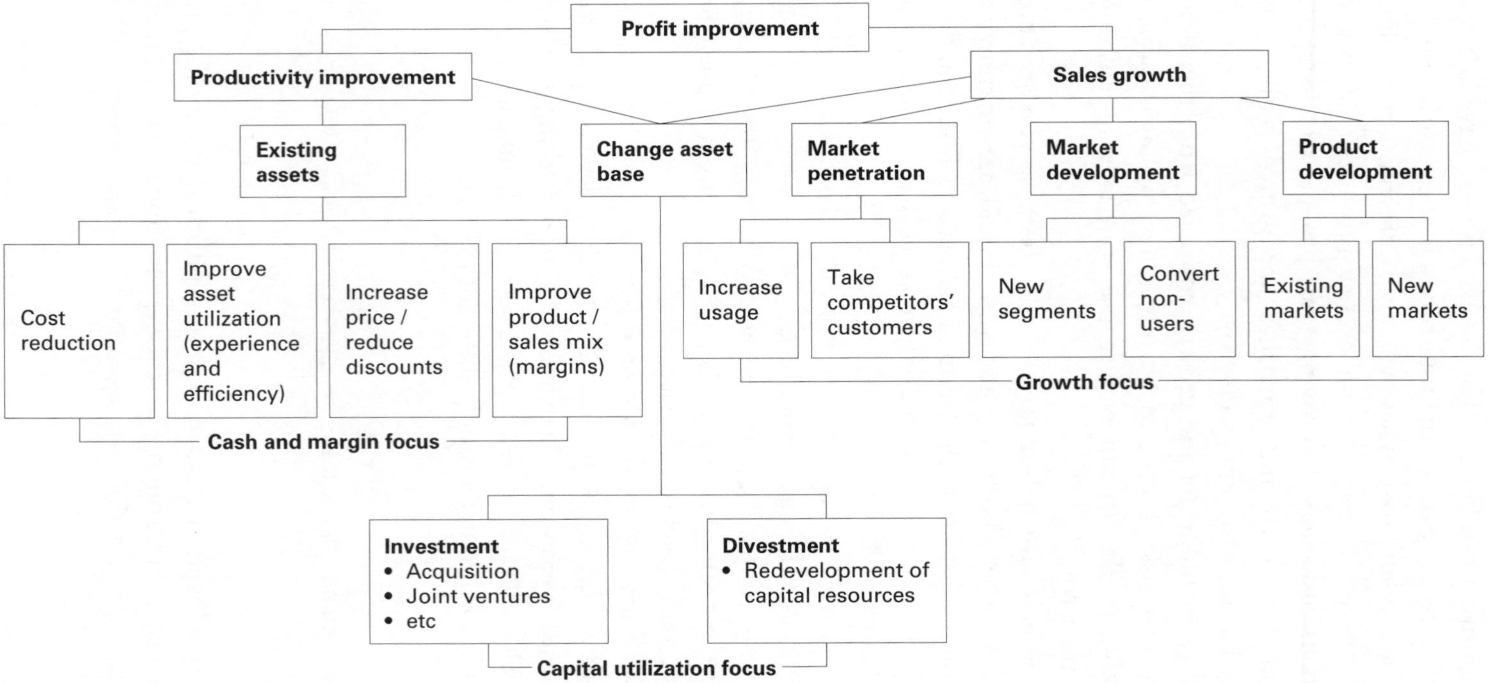

Profit improvement

Productivity improvement

Sales growth

Existing assets

Change asset base

Market penetration

Market development

Product development

Cost reduction

Improve asset utilization (experience and efficiency)

Increase price / reduce discounts

Improve product / sales mix (margins)

Increase usage

Take competitors' customers

New segments

Convert non-users

Existing markets

New markets

Growth focus

Cash and margin focus

Investment
- Acquisition
- Joint ventures
- etc

Divestment
- Redevelopment of capital resources

Capital utilization focus

Actions

As explained at the end of Chapter 1, you can now start planning your business future and templates are provided here for this purpose.

Figures 4.10 and 4.11 can now be completed. Let me stress that there are two exercises here – one for revenue and one for profit, and they should be completed separately.

One final important point

This gap analysis exercise should be completed by a small team of senior managers, preferably led by the CEO. It should not take longer than a couple of hours. The major advantage of doing this exercise **before** attempting to write a strategic marketing plan is that it sets out in clear relief the **shape** of future strategy and where the company's major efforts will have to be deployed.

It most definitely is **not** a strategic marketing plan and does **not** spell out how these revenues and profits are to be achieved. That is the purpose of the strategic marketing plan.

From here on, this book will spell out how to produce a strategic marketing plan, step by step.

Figure 4.10 Strategic Planning Exercise (Gap Analysis) 1 Revenue

1. OBJECTIVE

(A) Start by plotting the sales position you wish to achieve at the end of the planning period, point E.

(B) Next plot the forecast revenue position, point A

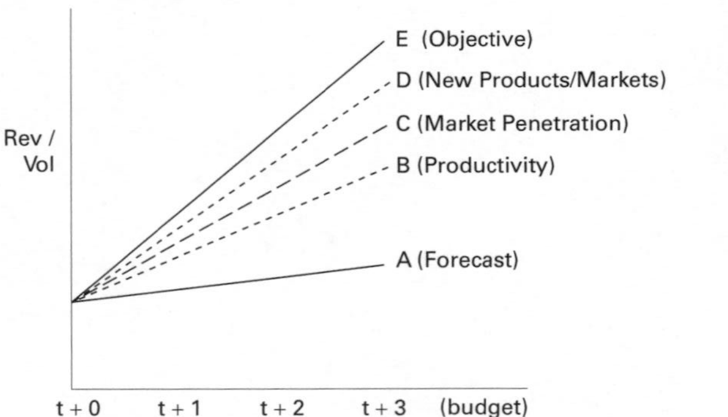

2. GAP ANALYSIS (Productivity)

Are there any actions you can take to close the gap under the following headings? Plot the total value of these on the Gap Analysis Graph on the left, point B. (These represent cash and margin focus). Now proceed to 3 below.

Productivity (NB: Not all factors are mutually exclusive)	Revenue
Better Product Mix (1)	
Better Customer Mix (2)	
More Sales Calls (3)	
Better Sales Calls (4)	
Increase Price	
Reduce Discounts	
Charge For Deliveries	
Total	

5. GAPANALYSIS
(Diversification)

Finally, list the value of any new products you might develop for new markets until point E is reached. (Steps 3, 4 and 5 represent a sales growth focus).

6. GAPANALYSIS
(Capital utilization)

If none of this gives the required return on investment consider changing the asset base. This could be

(A) Acquisition

(B) Joint Venture

(Step 6 represents a capital utilization focus)

Product 1, Product 2, Product 3, Etc

Market 1, Market 2, Market 3, Etc

3. GAPANALYSIS

ANSOFF PRODUCT/MARKET (MARKET PENETRATION)

(A) List principal products on the horizontal axis and principal markets on the vertical axis. In each smaller square write in current sales and achievable sales value during the planning period.

(B) Next, plot the market penetration position, point C. This point will be the addition of all the values in the right hand half of the small boxes in the Ansoff Matrix. If there is a gap, proceed to 4 below. Please note, revenue from (1) (2) (3) and (4) from the productivity box should be deducted from the market penetration total before plotting point C.

4. GAPANALYSIS

ANSOFF PRODUCT/MARKET MATRIX (NEW PRODUCTS/ NEW MARKETS)

Next, list the value of any new products you might develop which you might sell to existing markets. Alternatively, or as well as, if necessary, list the value of any existing products that you might sell to new markets. Plot the total value of these on the Gap Analysis Graph above, point D. If there is still a gap proceed to 5.

Product 1, Product 2, Product 3, Etc, Product 10, Product 11, Product 12, Etc

Market 1, Market 2, Market 3, Market 10, Market 11, Market 12, Etc

Figure 4.11 Strategic Planning Exercise (Gap Analysis) 2 Profit

1. OBJECTIVE

(A) Start by plotting the sales position you wish to achieve at the end of the planning period, point E.

(B) Next plot the forecast revenue position, point A

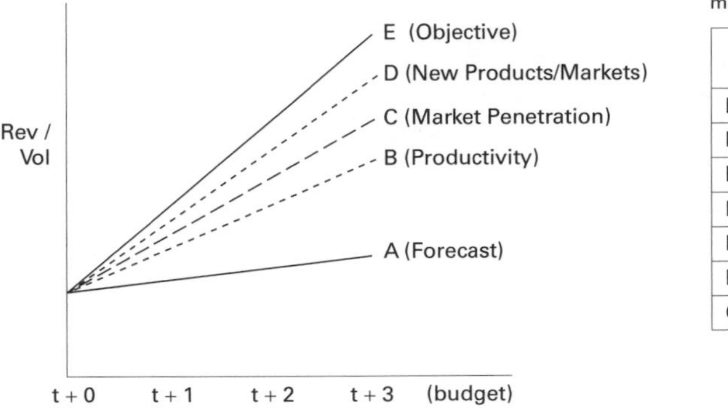

2. GAP ANALYSIS (Productivity)

Are there any actions you can take to close the gap under the following headings? Plot the total value of these on the Gap Analysis Graph on the left, point B. (These represent cash and margin focus). Now proceed to 3 below.

Productivity (NB: Not all factors are mutually exclusive)	Revenue
Better Product Mix (1)	
Better Customer Mix (2)	
More Sales Calls (3)	
Better Sales Calls (4)	
Increase Price	
Reduce Discounts	
Charge For Deliveries	
Total	

5. GAPANALYSIS
(Diversification)

Finally, list the value of any new products you might develop for new markets until point E is reached. (Steps 3, 4 and 5 represent a sales growth focus).

6. GAPANALYSIS
(Capital utilization)

If none of this gives the required return on investment consider changing the asset base. This could be

(A) Acquisition

(B) Joint Venture

(Step 6 represents a capital utilization focus)

3. GAPANALYSIS

ANSOFF PRODUCT/MARKET (MARKET PENETRATION)

(A) List principal products on the horizontal axis and principal markets on the vertical axis. In each smaller square write in current sales and achievable sales value during the planning period.

(B) Next, plot the market penetration position, point C. This point will be the addition of all the values in the right hand half of the small boxes in the Ansoff Matrix. If there is a gap, proceed to 4 below. Please note, revenue from (1) (2) (3) and (4) from the productivity box should be deducted from the market penetration total before plotting point C.

4. GAPANALYSIS

ANSOFF PRODUCT/MARKET MATRIX (NEW PRODUCTS/ NEW MARKETS)

Next, list the value of any new products you might develop which you might sell to existing markets. Alternatively, or as well as, if necessary, list the value of any existing products that you might sell to new markets. Plot the total value of these on the Gap Analysis Graph above, point D. If there is still a gap proceed to 5.

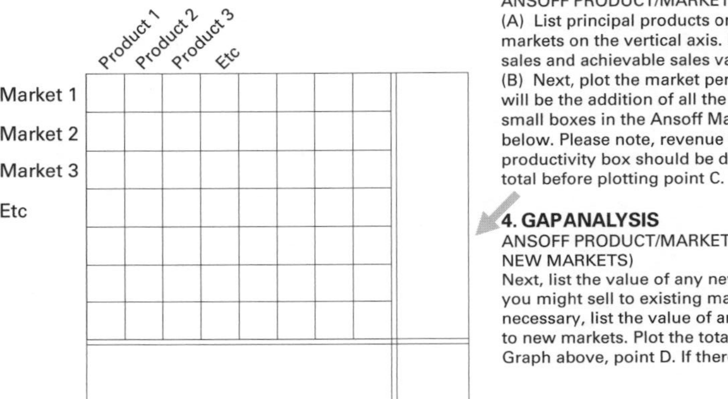

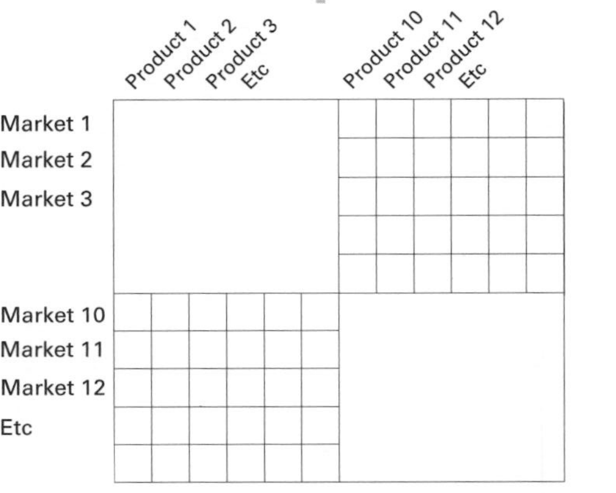

Market segmentation 05

Crucial to understanding your market and how it works

An important note from the author

I promise you, dear reader, that this is the only **difficult** chapter in the book. I have tried to make it as simple and practical as possible. Can I please ask you at least to read it, because market segmentation really is the key to commercial success.

If it is not possible to implement these core factors from the first few pages, I strongly recommend trying the 'Quick Market Segmentation Exercise' set out in Figures 16–20 at the end of this chapter. Thank you and good luck.

Introduction

We can now proceed to put together the first part of your strategic plan. Firstly, however, let me set out what the contents of your strategic plan should be. This chapter deals with the Market Overview section.

The contents of a Strategic Marketing Plan (T+3, fewer than 20 pages)

- Financial Summary
- Market Overview
  - how the market works
  - key segments and their needs
- SWOT Analyses of Segments
- Portfolio Summary of SWOTS
- Assumptions
- Objectives and Strategies
- Budget for Three Years

It is markets, the customers in these markets and their needs that must be focused on initially.

The first point to make is that it is a **strategic** plan covering a three-year period. The importance of strategy before tactics was spelled out in Chapter 2. Three years is the most frequent planning horizon for SMEs.

The second point to make is that the total document should be fewer than 20 pages when completed. If it can be reduced to around 10 pages, well and good, but it is important to note that if you can't spell out who you are selling to, their needs and why they should buy what you are offering rather than someone else's offer, together with the financial consequences in the strategy document, you are unlikely to achieve your objectives.

As I said in Chapter 1, whilst your products/services are important, it is **customers** and their **needs** that must be focused on initially and this is what this chapter is about. Please note, however, that whilst I am going to focus on markets and customers in this chapter, the first heading in the plan says: 'Financial Summary'. Clearly, this is the last thing you do after completing the plan, but it must be the **very first** thing that anyone reads (that is, people such as your investors, your board, your financial colleagues, etc). The reason is simple to understand.

Anyone will want to read on if they can instantly see what the plan is about. Just look at Figure 5.1.

Figure 5.1 Financial Summary

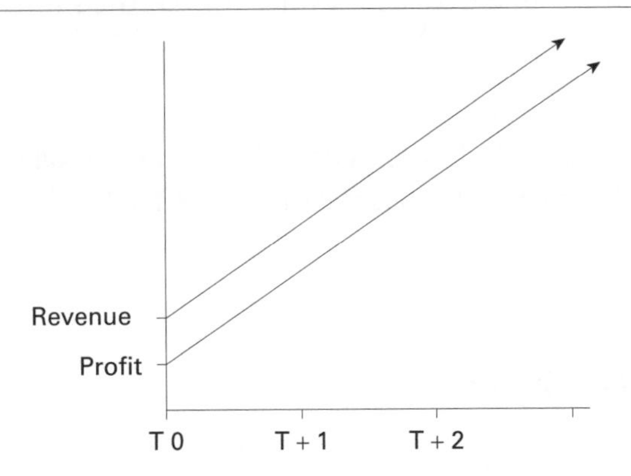

The following words, as an example, will entice anyone to want to read on:

> 'This plan shows revenue growing from £5 million to £10 million over the next three years and the profit growing from £500,000 to £1 million. The purpose of this strategic plan is to spell out how this will be achieved.'

These are, indeed, exciting words, as long, of course, as the subsequent plan actually does spell out clearly and simply how these results will be achieved.

> *The financial summary, which should be done last is the first thing executives will read. It should be clear and simple and inspire them to want to read on.*

Market overview

This is in four parts:

- what the market is;
- how it works;
- who the key decision makers are;
- how they are segmented, as they are not all the same.

A market is the total of all products and services which customers perceive as being capable of satisfying the same need.

What the market is

Whilst I am determined not to be overly 'academic', it is nonetheless necessary to dispel some very basic misconceptions about markets. In Chapter 1, I spelled out some of the disasters that resulted from companies thinking of their markets in terms of **products** (IBM – mainframes, Gestetner – duplicators, Kodak – cameras and film, Nokia – phones, etc). My personal definition of a market is: 'the aggregation of all the alternative products or services which customers regard as being capable of satisfying that same need'. Table 5.1 is an example of the financial services market. Take a product like **pensions**. This fits clearly into the 'retirement income' market. But there are lots of other products that satisfy the same need, so it is essential to understand what these other products are.

Another example is the market for books on marketing.

Redefining the market for books totally changed the board's approach to its markets.

Table 5.1 Some key market definitions (personal market)

Market	Need
Emergency Cash ('Rainy Day')	Cash to cover an undesired and unexpected event (often the loss of/damage to property)
Future Event Planning	Schemes to protect and grow money that are for anticipated and unanticipated cash-calling events (eg car replacement/repairs, education, weddings, funerals, healthcare)
Asset Purchase	Cash to buy assets they require (eg car purchase, house purchase, once-in-a-lifetime holiday)
Welfare Contingency	The ability to maintain a desired standard of living (for self and/or dependants) in times of unplanned cessation of salary
Retirement Income	The ability to maintain a desired standard of living (for self and/or dependants) once the salary cheques have ceased
Wealthcare and Building	The care and growth of assets (with various risk levels and liquidity levels)
Day-to-day Money Management	Ability to store and readily access cash for day-to-day requirements
Personal Financial Protection and Security from Motor Vehicle Incidents	Currently known as car insurance

I spent a day with the board of a book publisher and we took marketing books as an example. Figure 5.2 shows their first effort at a market map. Figure 5.3, however, shows a much broader market definition – in this case 'the promulgation of knowledge about marketing'. It can be seen that the broader definition encapsulated many different ways of promulgating marketing knowledge. This completely changed the board's approach to its markets. Whilst books were still an important part of this, many other profitable avenues opened up for them. More importantly, they discovered why the market for marketing books was shrinking and were able to take advantage of new opportunities.

Figure 5.2 Market map for marketing books

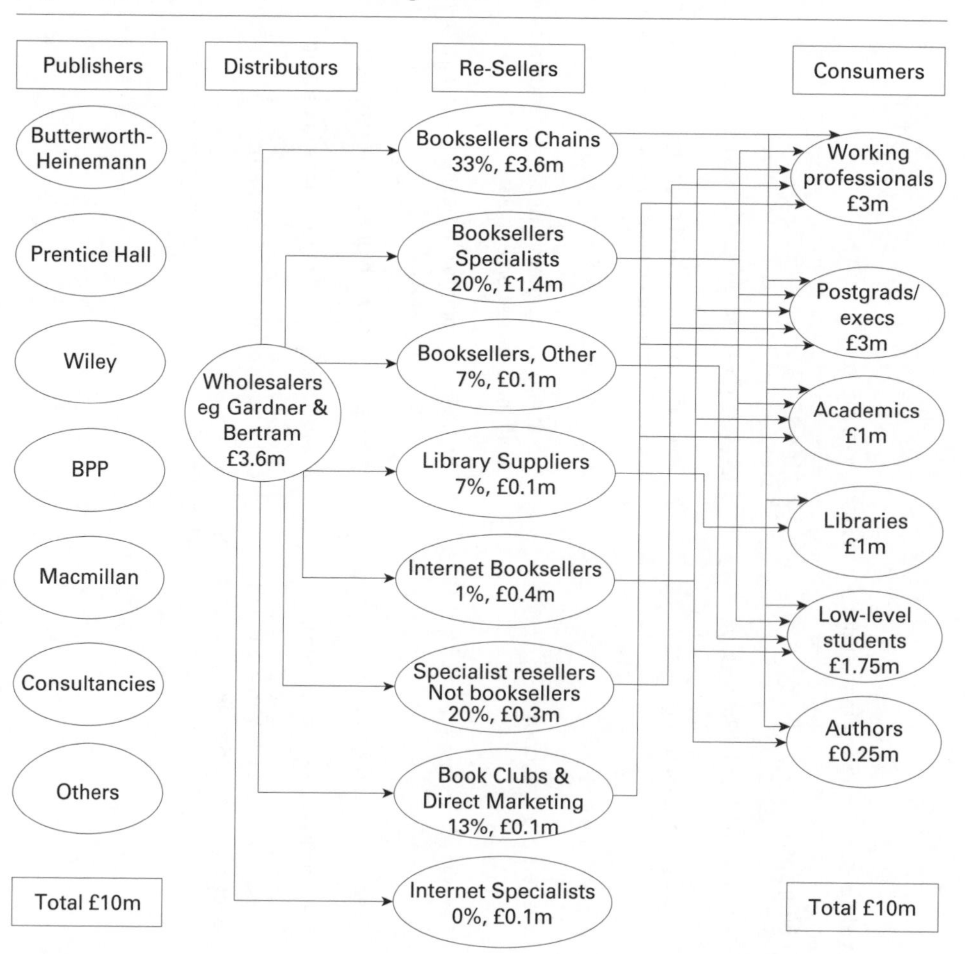

Figure 5.3 Market map for marketing knowledge promulgation

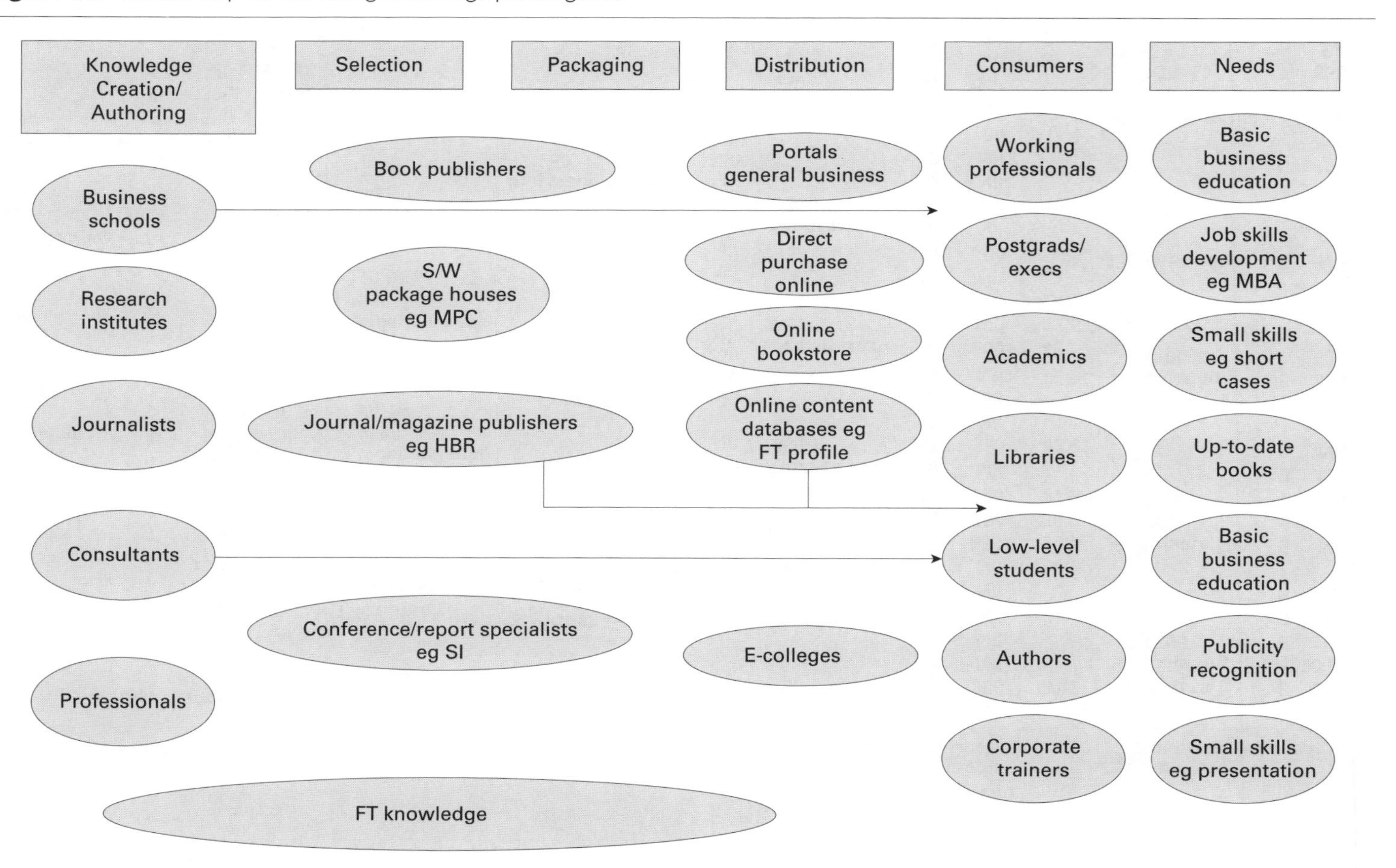

Figure 5.4 Radiator market map

Radiator Manufacturer

Manufacturer	Distribution		Sector Share
Stelrad	1	1830	70.2
2275	2	360	17.3
41.7%	3	66	11.2
	4	Nil	Nil
Premier	1	555	21.3
860	2	280	12.8
15.8%	3	26	4.3
	4	Nil	Nil
Supaline	1	125	4.8
605	2	450	20.5
11.1%	3	30	5.1
	4	Nil	Nil
Barlo	1	90	3.4
480	2	270	12.3
8.8%	3	120	20.7
	4	Nil	Nil
Warmastyle	1	5	Nil
300	2	255	11.6
5.5%	3	40	6.9
	4	Nil	Nil
Other Imports	1	Nil	Nil
905	2	556	25.3
17.1%	3	300	51.8
	4	80	100.0
5.4 million			

Distributor

Distributor
1. National Merchants 2605 47.8%
2. Large Independents 2190 40.1%
3. Small Independents 560 10.6%
4. Sheds 80 1.4%
5.4 million

Installer

Installer		
5. British Gas	1	295
465	2	170
8.5%	3	Nil
	4	Nil
6. Installer	1	1065
2755	2	1360
50.5%	3	360
	4	Nil
7. Contractor	1	1135
1905	2	540
34.9%	3	230
	4	Nil
8. Self Installer	1	Nil
80	2	Nil
1.4%	3	Nil
	4	80
9. Direct Works	1	120
250	2	130
4.6%	3	Nil
	4	Nil
5.4 million		

Primary Leverage Point

Specification Decision

Specification Decision			
Manufacturer	10	Nil	
250	11	250	31.3
	12	Nil	
	13	Nil	
	14	Nil	
Local Authority	10	Nil	
	11	Nil	
1350	12	1050	95.4
	13	50	50.0
	14	250	27.8
Housebuilder	10	Nil	
350	11	350	43.8
	12	Nil	
	13	Nil	
	14	Nil	
British Gas	10	500	19.6
700	11	100	12.5
	12	50	4.5
	13	Nil	
	14	50	5.6
Contractor	10	Nil	
200	11	100	12.5
	12	Nil	
	13	Nil	
	14	100	11.1
Consultant	10	Nil	
550	11	Nil	
	12	Nil	
	13	50	50.1
	14	500	55.6
3.4 million			**623**

End User Segment

End User Segment		
10. Private Exitsting	5	385
	6	2010
2555	7	100
46.8%	8	80
	9	Nil
11. Private New	5	Nil
800	6	50
14.7%	7	750
	8	Nil
	9	Nil
12. Public Existing	5	50
	6	395
1100	7	506
20.2%	8	Nil
	9	150
13. Public New	5	Nil
100	6	Nil
1.8%	7	Nil
	8	Nil
	9	100
14. Commercial	5	50
900	6	300
16.5%	7	550
	8	Nil
	9	Nil
5.4 million		

All right, if you don't want to go down this route, I don't mind, but please be careful that you don't fall into the common 'product' trap. You will, of course, still depend on your products or services for making money, so you now need to try to understand how the market works for these specifically.

How the market works: market mapping

In any market, 100 per cent of goods/services are 'made', distributed and bought, and it is essential to know what is happening out there in that particular market.

Let me give you an example of a market map for radiators. Figure 5.4 is the very first attempt this comparatively small company made to quantify its market.

From this – in summary – it can be seen that 5.4 million radiators were either made here or were imported, 5.4 million radiators were distributed, 5.4 million radiators were specified and 5.4 million radiators ended up on a wall somewhere. In other words, it **balanced**!

The only problem was that, whilst it told them a lot about distributors and the like, there was a big black hole in the penultimate column (which shows that only the decision makers for 3.4 million radiators had been identified). Subsequent research showed that **architects** were key specifiers of which radiators should be installed, but up to this point, they weren't considered to be 'customers'; because architects didn't buy radiators. From then on, however, since they accounted for about 35 per cent of the market, they became a primary focus of this radiator manufacturer. Fifteen years later, this particular company is the market leader!

In reality, market maps don't have to be all that complicated and as long as you know **approximately** how it works, this should be sufficient.

A market map, like a balance sheet, should 'balance' what is sold with what is bought throughout the value chain.

Figure 5.5 illustrates a much simpler form of market mapping. At the end of this chapter is a format for you to complete your own, simple market map. Guidelines on how to draw a market map are also given later in this chapter in Figure 5.22.

Figure 5.5 Identifying the decision makers

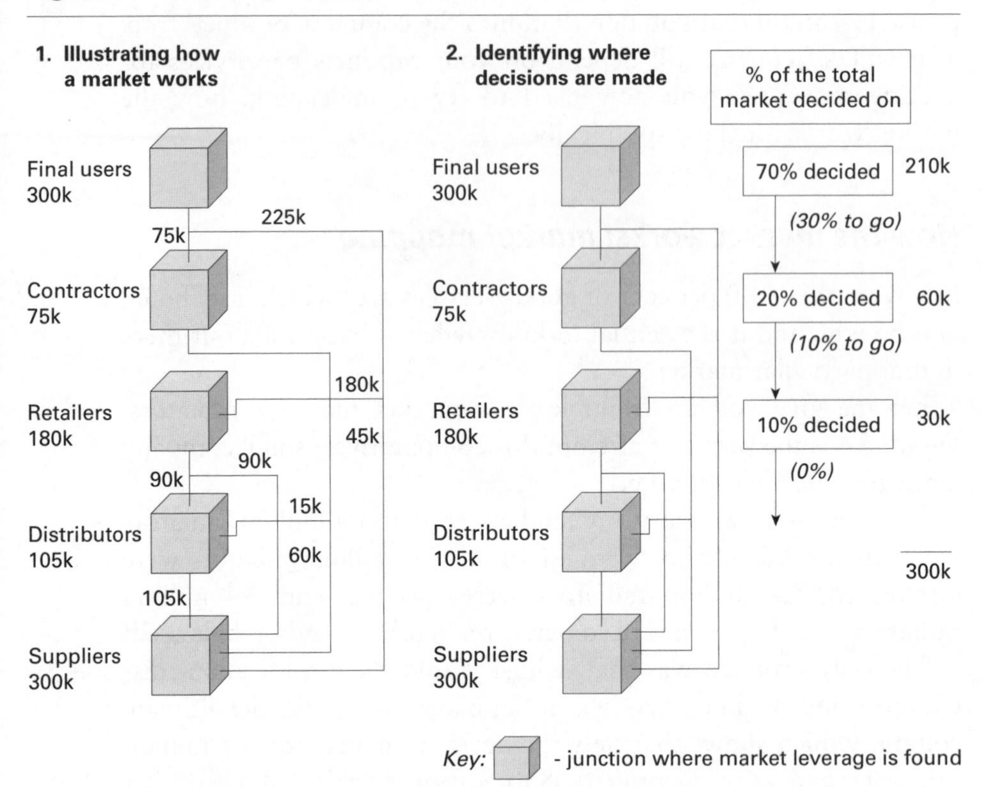

SOURCE: Extract from McDonald and Dunbar (2012) *Market Segmentation: How to do it, how to profit from it*, Wiley

Market segmentation is the bedrock of successful commercial enterprises.

Who the key decision makers are

The easiest junction to start the market map is the final user's junction, noting at each junction the volume/value (or percentage of the total market) decided there. Guesstimate these figures if they are not known. Figure 5.5 shows a market in which 30 per cent annual sales are decided at junctions other than at the final user junction, and it is at each of these important junctions that market segmentation should take place.

Referring back to Figure 5.4 and the architects example, although about 35 per cent of radiators are specified by architects, it must be pointed out that there is no such thing as an 'average' architect. They all behave differently and are unique in their own way, so some method has to be found of grouping them in such a way that it becomes possible to communicate with them effectively, that is, **segmenting** them.

There is no such thing as an average customer. They are all different, so some way has to be found of grouping like-minded customers together – this is called 'segmentation'.

Segmentation

If you have lost a bit of focus reading this chapter so far, don't despair, as in some cases, market mapping isn't essential.

Market segmentation, however, is essential, as it is the very cornerstone of successful business enterprise and this next section should be read very carefully and acted upon.

Over the years, scholars and consultants have sought to discover the secret of success and 137 separate pieces of research have identified the following as the cornerstone of success (references supplied on request). More than 40 years of research into the link between long-run financial success and excellent marketing strategies reveal the following:

Characteristics of successful marketing strategies

Excellent strategies	Weak strategies
• Understand markets in depth.	• Always talk about products.
• Target needs-based segments.	• Target product categories.
• Make a specific offer to each segment.	• Make similar offers to all segments.
• Have clear differentiation, positioning and branding.	• Have no differentiation and poor positioning and branding.
• Leverage their strengths and minimize their weaknesses.	• Have little understanding of their strengths and weaknesses.
• Anticipate the future.	• Plan using historical data.

Here, however, is the major problem, for most organizations do not understand segmentation and get it hopelessly wrong. Indeed, a recent *Harvard Business Review* article claimed that 85 per cent of new product launches in the United States failed simply because of poor market segmentation.

Most books incorrectly state that there are several bases for market segmentation, such as socio-economics, demographics, geodemographics and the like. But this misses the point totally. Boy George and the Archbishop of Canterbury are both socio-economic group A, but apart from wearing dresses and singing a lot, they don't behave the same! Nor do all 18–24-year-old females behave the same (demographics). Nor does everyone in my street (geodemographics) behave the same!

> *Market segmentation is NOT socio-economics, demographics or geodemographics.*

All goods and services in a sector are made, distributed, bought and used, and all the purchase combinations make up an **actual** market, so the task is to understand what these different purchase combinations – or segments – are.

Before explaining how to do this, let me examine the factors that cause markets to break into smaller groups by describing briefly how products/services get adopted in markets. Figure 5.6 illustrates what looks like a normal distribution curve.

Figure 5.6 Non-cumulative diffusion pattern

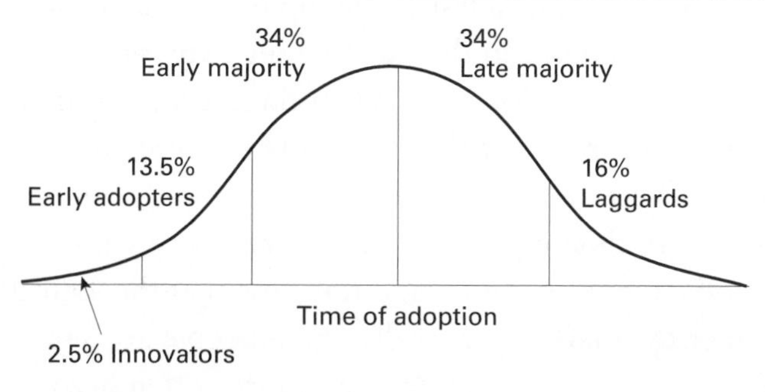

SOURCE: Adapted from Everett Rogers

When something new is invented such as television, computers, microwave ovens, the internet and the like, not everyone adopts them at the same time. Many years ago, a US researcher, called Everett Rogers, studied how new products are diffused across markets over time. Imagine that television has just been invented. Let us take any market, Germany will do, and let us imagine that there are only 100 households in Germany. Let us further imagine that there is a law limiting each household in Germany to only one television. Clearly, the potential market for televisions in Germany is 100, but not everyone buys one at the same time. Someone has to be the first to adopt new products. Normally, about 2.5 per cent of any population will be the first to adopt new products. These people are known as 'Innovators'. They are unusual people who enjoy being different.

> *Not everyone adopts new products and services at the same time. Understanding why this is so can be quite useful for business people.*

These people are followed by another group, known as 'Opinion Leaders' (called early adopters in Figure 5.6 – about 13.5 per cent of the market). These people tend to be affluent, are well-educated, very privileged, and they are independent thinkers, who do not care much what other people think of them. They are, however, crucial in getting any new product or service adopted. We can think of them as the Joneses, in the sense of the expression: 'Keeping up with the Joneses'.

This group is followed by a much larger group known as the 'Early Majority'. These people admire the opinion leaders and can be thought of as the Smiths, in the sense of the expression: 'The Smiths try to keep up with the Joneses'. When these people start to enter a market, there is a rapid growth in sales. (They represent about 34 per cent of the market).

By now, approximately 50 per cent of all those who could adopt the new product, have done so, and it is now that the 'Late Majority' begin to enter the market. Generally, these people are less privileged, less affluent, and less well-educated, and price often becomes important at this stage in the market.

Finally, the remaining 16 per cent of the population adopt the new technology. Rogers, (the originator of this research in 1976) referred to these people as 'Laggards'. By now, everyone who could have one has got one. For example, in the United Kingdom, everyone has a mobile phone, they are very cheap, and the market can now be considered to be a replacement market, in which growth will be dependent on population size, demographics and the like. Clearly, in mature markets, getting growth will be much more difficult.

Although this is not the purpose of this chapter, it is useful to note, before I leave Roger's diffusion of innovation curve, that when launching a new product or service, it is advantageous to know who the opinion leaders are in a market, as these people should be targeted first by the sales force, and by other promotional media, as they will be the most likely to respond. For example, certain doctors will be more open-minded about new drugs, whereas other doctors will not risk prescribing a new drug until it has been on the market for a number of years.

When launching a new product, it is useful to know who the 'opinion leaders' are, as these people will be more likely to buy.

The diffusion of innovation curve also explains the phenomenon known as the product life cycle, and why, after the 50 per cent point on the diffusion of innovation curve is reached, the market continues to grow, but the rate of growth begins to decline until maturity is reached. See Figure 5.7, which shows how the two curves relate to each other.

Figure 5.7 Generalized cumulative and non-cumulative diffusion

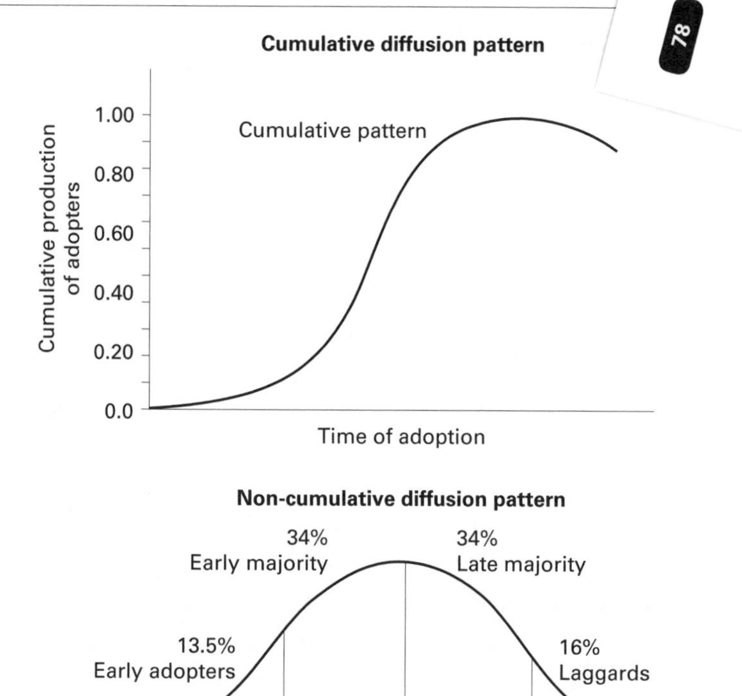

All this has been explained in order to introduce the key concept of market segmentation and why it happens. Clearly, in the early days, markets will tend to be homogeneous. But, as demand grows rapidly with the entry of the early majority, it is common for new entrants to offer variations on the early models, as I have just explained and consumers now have a choice. In order to explain this more clearly, let me illustrate the approximate shape of markets. If we were to plot the car market in terms of speed and price, we would see very small, inexpensive cars in the bottom left-hand corner (see Figure 5.8). In the top right, we would see very fast, expensive cars. Most cars, however, would cluster in the middle, what we might call: 'The Mr and Mrs Average' market.

The biggest part of most markets is the 'Mr and Mrs Average' in the middle.

…igure 5.8 Representation of the car market

Similarly, the lawn mower market would look very similar (see Figure 5.9). With lawn size on the vertical axis and price on the horizontal axis, at the bottom left would be small, inexpensive, hand-pushed mowers, with expensive sit-on machines for large estates in the right-hand corner. That leaves the mass of the market with average size lawns, and average size lawn mowers, which is where the mass market is.

Figure 5.9 Representation of the lawn mower market

We can now redraw this to represent the shape of any market, particularly at the early growth stage (the shape on the left in

Figure 5.10). But when rapid growth begins, new entrants join the market and offer variations on standard products in order to attract sales, and it is at this stage that markets begin to break into smaller groups, whilst still growing overall. (This is represented by the shape in the middle.) Eventually, when markets mature, and there is more supply than demand, any market growth tends to come in the lower price end of the market, whilst the top end of the market tends to be immune. (This is represented by the shape on the right.) It is usually the middle market that suffers at this stage, with many competitors vying with each other on price. This, however, is the whole point of market segmentation, for competing only on price is to assume that this is the main requirement of customers, whereas the truth is that this is rarely the case. It is just that a general lack of understanding about market segmentation on the part of suppliers about the real needs of customers in mature markets, forces them to trade on price, so encouraging the market to become a commodity market.

It is when markets become mature that suppliers who do not understand segmentation have to drop their prices.

Figure 5.10 The development of market shape from birth to maturity

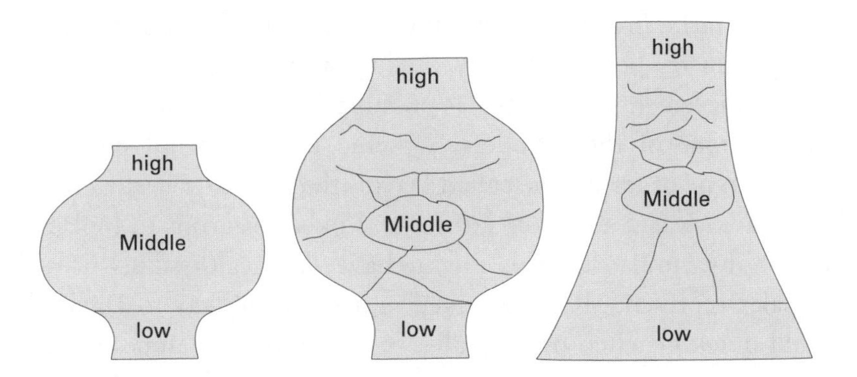

A fertilizer company that had grown and prospered during the 1970s and 1980s, because of the superior nature of its products, reached its farmer consumers via merchants (wholesalers). However, as other

companies copied the technology, the merchants began to stock competitive products and drove prices and margins down. Had the fertilizer company paid more attention to the needs of its different farmer groups and developed products especially for them, based on farmer segmentation, it would have continued to create demand pull-through differentiation.

Competitors can copy products, but they can't copy your relationship with customers.

The segmentation study revealed that there were seven distinct types of farmer, each with a different set of needs. To give just three examples of these segments, see Figure 5.11. Firstly, there was a segment we called Arthur (the character in the top middle), a television character known for his deals. He bought on price alone but represented only 10 per cent of the market, not the 100 per cent put about by everyone in the industry, especially the sales force. Another type of farmer we called Oliver (the character in the bottom right of the figure). Oliver would drive around his fields on his tractor with an aerial linked to a satellite and an on-board computer. He did this in order to analyse the soil type and would then mix P, N and K, which are the principal ingredients of fertilizer, in order to get the maximum yield out of his farm. In other words, Oliver was a scientific farmer, but the supply industry believed he was buying on price because he bought his own ingredients as cheaply as possible. He did this, however, only because none of the suppliers bothered to understand his needs. Another type of farmer we called David (the character in the bottom left). David was a show-off farmer and liked his crops to look nice and healthy. He also liked his cows to have nice, healthy skins. Clearly, if a sales representative had talked in a technical way to David, he would quickly switch off. Equally, to talk about the appearance of crops and livestock would have switched Oliver off, but this is the whole point. Every single supplier in the industry totally ignored the real needs of these farmers, and the only thing anyone ever talked about was price. The result: A market driven by price discounts, accompanied by substantial losses to the suppliers. This company, however, armed with this new found information, launched new products and new promotional approaches aimed at these different farmer types, and got immediate results, becoming the most profitable subsidiary of the parent company and the only profitable fertilizer company in Europe.

Figure 5.11 Personalizing segments

The whole industry ignored the real needs of farmers and consequently talked only about price.

One more example should convince you of the crucial importance of market segmentation. Table 5.2 shows on the right what an IT company used to put in its brochures, which was essentially the same as all suppliers. Figure 5.12, however, shows nine segments of IT buyers, all clearly different. Armed with this knowledge, this company surged ahead of all its competitors and became the market leader and very profitable.

Table 5.2 Listen to how customers talk about category need

Customer View	Supplier View
Advice	Fast PAD family
Cutting costs	Multimedia FRADs
Future technology direction	PIX firewall
Help	
Design and configuration	Solutions
Process engineering	Gigabit Ethernet solutions
Electron commerce	
Run	High Performance
International network	LAN Support
Disaster recovery	

Figure 5.12 Understand the different category buyers

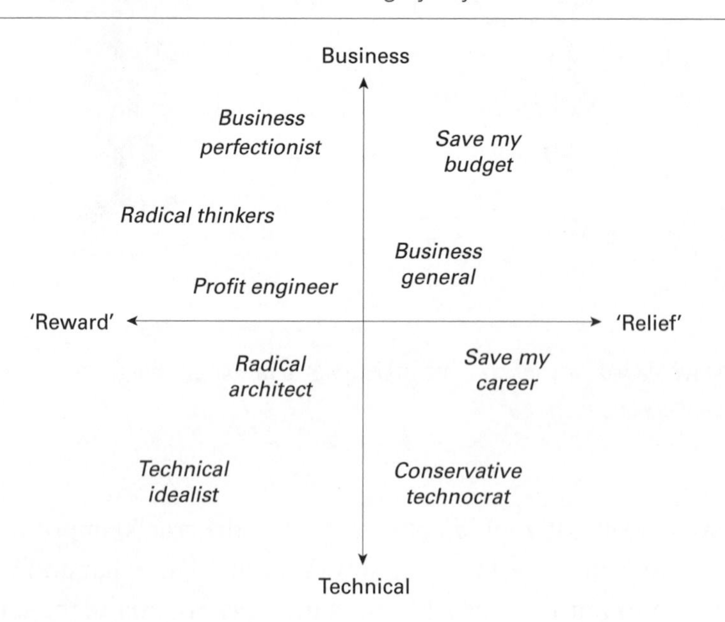

I can now proceed to explain market segmentation and how to do it.

Getting started

To get started, we need to develop a representative sample of different decision makers, what I refer to as 'micro segments'. The principle behind this step is that by observing the purchase behaviour of decision makers, we have a platform for developing a detailed understanding of their motivations, which in turn becomes the basis on which segments are formed.

Table 5.3 is a template for attempting this exercise. Although it shows only 10 micro segments, most companies can easily identify at least 20 micro segments. Remember, these micro segments are actual purchase combinations that take place in a market.

Table 5.4 is a summarized example of a finished segmentation project for the toothpaste market.

We need to understand as many combinations as possible of actual purchase patterns in the market.

If you have difficulty answering the 'why' question, you may need to carry out elementary market research, but in my experience, most SMEs are clever enough and experienced enough to be able to answer the question.

Table 5.3 Micro segments

Micro segment	1	2	3	4	5	6	7	8	9	10
What is bought										
Where										
When										
How										
Who										
Why (benefits sought)										

Table 5.4 Segmentation in the toothpaste market

	Segment Name	Worrier	Sociable	Sensory	Independent
Who buys	Socio-economic	C1 C2	B C1 C2	C1 C2 D	A B
	Demographics	Large families 25–40	Teens Young Smokers	Children	Males 35–50
	Psychographics	conservative hypochondriasis	high sociability: active	high self-involvement: hedonists	high autonomy value oriented
What is bought	% of total market	50%	30%	15%	5%
	Product examples	Crest	McLeans Ultra Bright	Colgate (stripe)	Own label
	Product physics	large canisters	large tubes	medium tubes	small tubes
	Price paid	low	high	medium	low
	Outlet	supermarket	supermarket	supermarket	independent
	Purchase frequency	weekly	monthly	monthly	quarterly
Why	Benefits sought	stop decay	attract attention	flavour	functionality
Potential for growth		nil	high	medium	nil

To summarize so far, it is clear that no market is totally homogeneous (see Figure 5.13).

Figure 5.13 An undifferentiated market

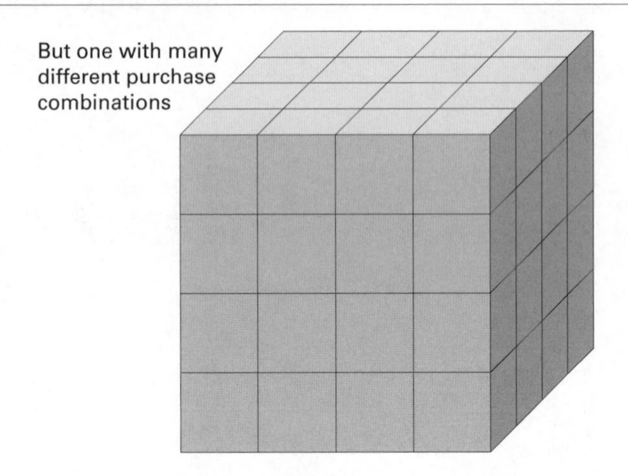

The reality is that actual markets consist of a large number of different purchase combinations (see Figure 5.14).

Figure 5.14 Different needs in a market

However, as it is impracticable to deal with more than between seven and 10, a process has to be found to bring together, or cluster, all those micro segments that share similar needs (see Figure 5.15), something that any good computer program can do.

Figure 5.15 Segments in a market

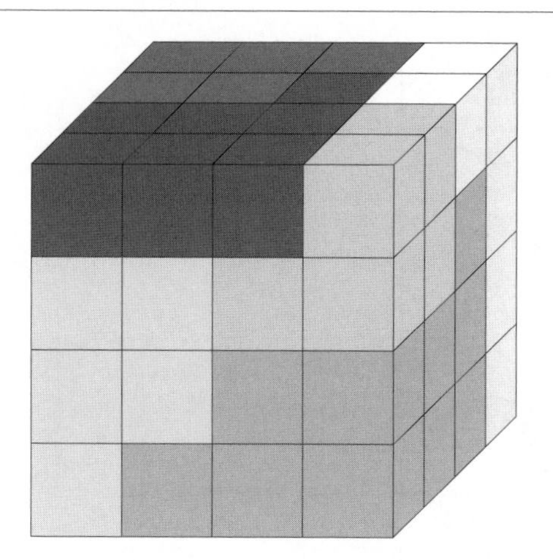

A shortcut method

Not everyone will want go through this rigorous process described above, so I have developed a short cut, which any reader should easily be able to implement.

Start by completing the product/market table (Table 5.5). As explained earlier, just concentrate on the five or six boxes that account for about 80 per cent of your turnover. Take each of these in turn and then follow the process described in Figures 5.16–5.20.

1. Select a business unit, or part of the business, for which you wish to develop a partial plan. Business unit: ____________________
2. Along the top of the table, list the principal products, product groups or services sold by the business unit, ignoring unimportant ones.
3. Down the left of the table, list the principal markets, or market segments, you sell into, ignoring unimportant ones.
4. Now choose four to six product-markets (cells) to concentrate on. For each, estimate your current revenue in the box.

Table 5.5 Product-market table

Products: / Markets:	1:	2:	3:	4:	5:	6:	7:
1:							
2:							
3:							
4:							
5:							
6:							
7:							

Although this is not as thorough as the process described above, it should enable you to develop a number of actionable market segments.

In conclusion, whatever you do, please don't lose heart if you have found this chapter hard going. Even if you can't follow my methods to develop segments, as long as you understand the principle involved, just have a go at generating some segments intuitively and this will be better than marmalading your efforts over some mythical, average customer, as, eventually, this will inevitably force you to compete on price as a 'pimply little me-too'.

Quick Market Segmentation Exercise

- Write down the **main** benefits sought by customers.
- Hygiene factors are benefits that any product or service must have to be acceptable in the market. Try to ignore these.
- Motivators are those benefits that contribute towards the customer's decision about which product to buy.
- Take the 'motivators' and choose the two main ones.
- Draw two straight horizontal lines and make an estimate of the percentage of customers at each end. So, for example, if service level is a key motivator of what is bought:

Figure 5.16a

40% Low service ———————— 60% High service

Likewise, if the breadth of the product range is a key motivator of what is bought:

Figure 5.16b

40% Low range ———————— 60% High range

- Take the left-hand point of the first horizontal line and drag it over the second horizontal line to make a cross as shown in Figure 5.17.

Figure 5.17 Quick Market Segmentation Exercise

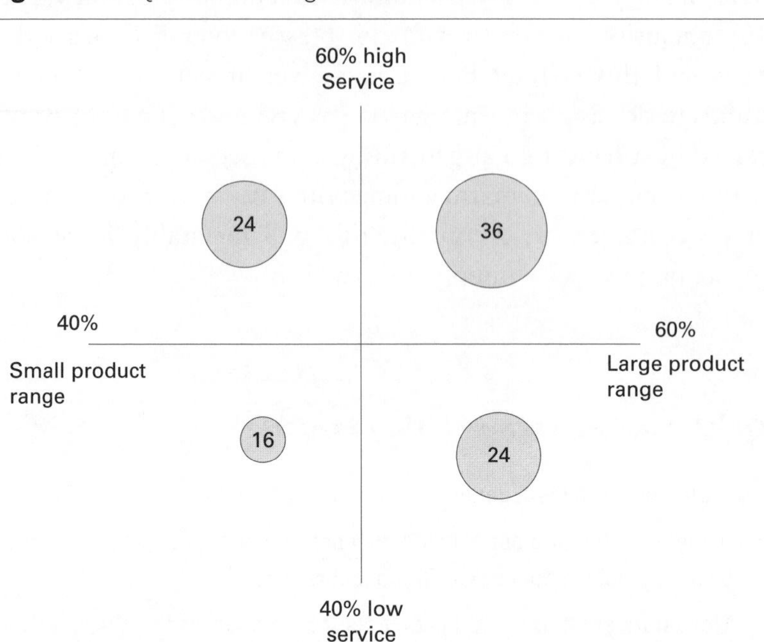

- Starting at the top, and moving in a clockwise direction, multiply 60% by 60% to give 36% (see first circle).
- Then multiply 60% by 40% to give 24% (see second circle).
- Then multiply 40% (the bottom of the vertical axis) by 40% to give 16% (see third circle).
- Lastly, multiply 40% by 40% to give 16% (see fourth circle).
- The circles represent segments in the market.

The resulting segments

Interpetation

- The first segment (36%), the biggest segment, requires both high service and a large product range.
- The second segment (24%) prefers a large product range and is less interested in service.
- The third segment (16%), doesn't care much about either a large product range or service.

- The fourth segment (24%) prefers good service and is less interested in a large product range.
- Although not essential, you might consider giving each segment a name.

Action

- Ensure your 'offer', including the product, price, service and promotion reflect the differing needs of each segment.

Example

- An example of segmentation of the A4 paper market follows. Please note that if, as in the case of the A4 paper market, there is one very large segment (in this case 56%), the exercise can be repeated for just this large segment, resulting in seven segments in total (Figure 5.18).

Example: Copier paper

- **Service** delivery (fast, paper always 'there' – point of delivery availability of products; service levels).
- **Product fit for purpose** (high-quality print finish for colour copiers; consistency of quality; paper that doesn't screw up in the machine; print definition; no waste).
- **Environmental factors** (recyclable).
- **Level of support** (delivered in small lots; consignment stock; easy ordering online; delivered to difficult locations).

Figure 5.18 Example of segmentation of a market

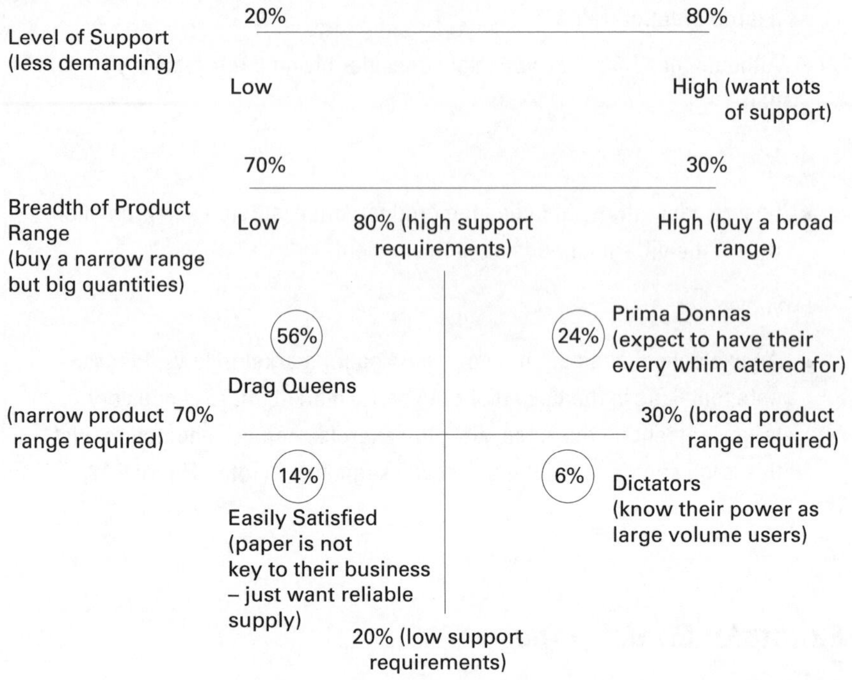

Actions

Important note: Please remember the contents of a strategic plan for what you sell and who you sell it to, shown again opposite. Please note that the finished plan should be fewer than 20 pages and fewer if possible.

The contents of a Strategic Marketing Plan (T+3, fewer than 20 pages)

- Financial Summary
- Market Overview
  - how the market works
  - key segments and their needs
- SWOT Analyses of Segments
- Portfolio Summary of SWOTS
- Assumptions
- Objectives and Strategies
- Budget for Three Years

Now I am going to explain how to do the first section ('Financial Summary') and the second section ('Market Overview – in two parts – how the market works' and 'key segments and their needs').

Financial Summary

Figures 5.19 and 5.20 show what should appear first in the strategic plan.

Figure 5.19 The contents of the Strategic Marketing Plan

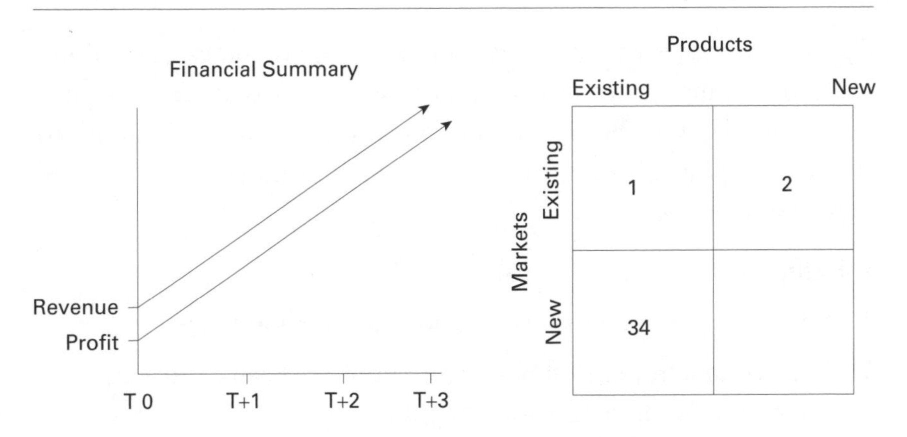

Key (revenue and profit growth)

- from productivity
  - by product for market for existing products from existing markets;
- from new products in existing markets;
- from existing products in new markets;
- from new products in new markets.

Plus a few words of commentary.

Market Overview/Summary

- Market definition.
- Market map showing volume/revenue flows from supplier through to end user, with major decision points highlighted.
- Where appropriate, provide a future market map.
- Include commentary/conclusions/implications for the company.
- At major decision points, include key segments.

Please note, however, that you are going to have to delay doing this until you have completed your plan. So we now proceed to the 'Market Overview' section of the plan, as explained in this chapter.

Market overview

Figure 5.20 shows how to draw a market map. If you can't (or don't want to) do this, at the very least write some words about how your market works. On the assumption, however, that you are going to attempt this crucial section of your strategic plan, please follow the suggested process:

1. Define your market.
2. Draw a market map using the guidelines in Figure 5.20.
3. Show volume/revenue flows from supplier through to end user, with major decision points highlighted.

Figure 5.20 Market mapping

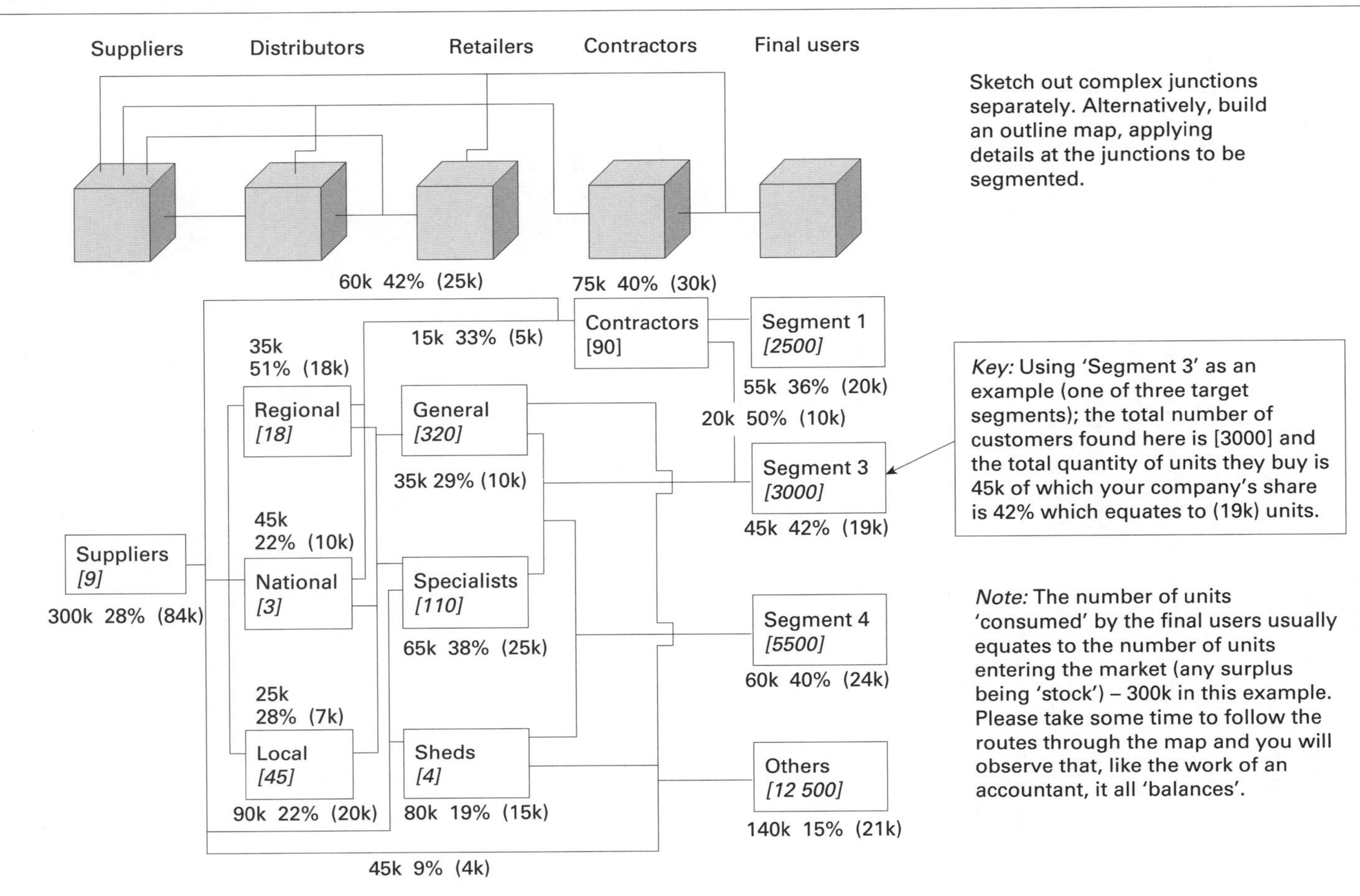

Sketch out complex junctions separately. Alternatively, build an outline map, applying details at the junctions to be segmented.

Key: Using 'Segment 3' as an example (one of three target segments); the total number of customers found here is [3000] and the total quantity of units they buy is 45k of which your company's share is 42% which equates to (19k) units.

Note: The number of units 'consumed' by the final users usually equates to the number of units entering the market (any surplus being 'stock') – 300k in this example. Please take some time to follow the routes through the map and you will observe that, like the work of an accountant, it all 'balances'.

4. Where appropriate, provide a future market map.
5. Include comments/conclusions/implications for your company.
6. At major decision points, include key segments – these are the result of your analysis above.

Figure 5.21 shows a market map sketched by some directors of a distributor (builder's merchant), and included is a template (Figure 5.22) so you can have a go at doing this.

This concludes the first section of your strategic plan. In Chapter 6, I will proceed to show you how to ascertain the needs of customers in the segments you have identified as a result of your analysis in this chapter.

Figure 5.21 Internal wall covering market map as sketched by the directors of a distributor

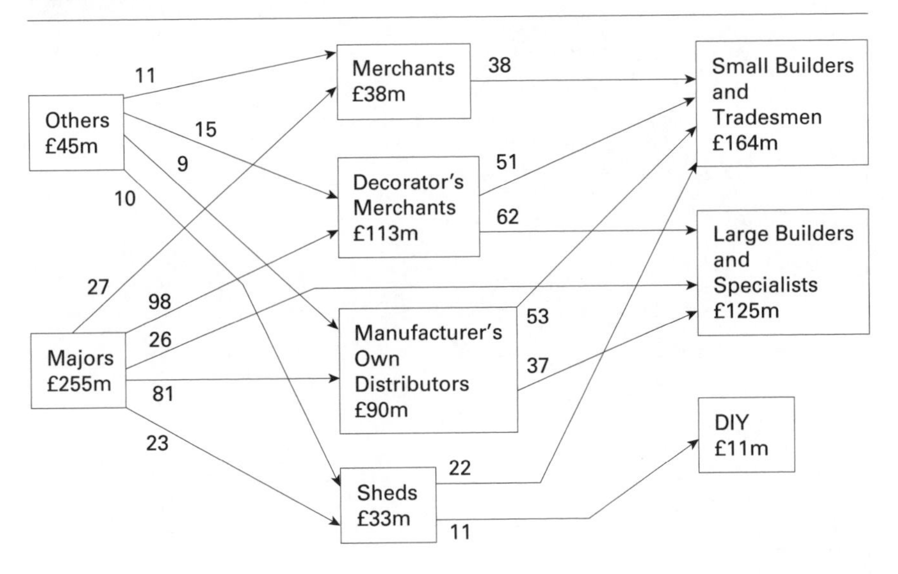

Figure 5.22 Template for your own market map

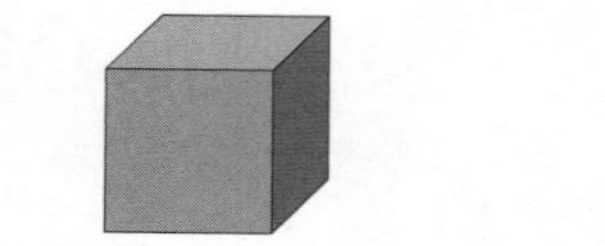

Example:

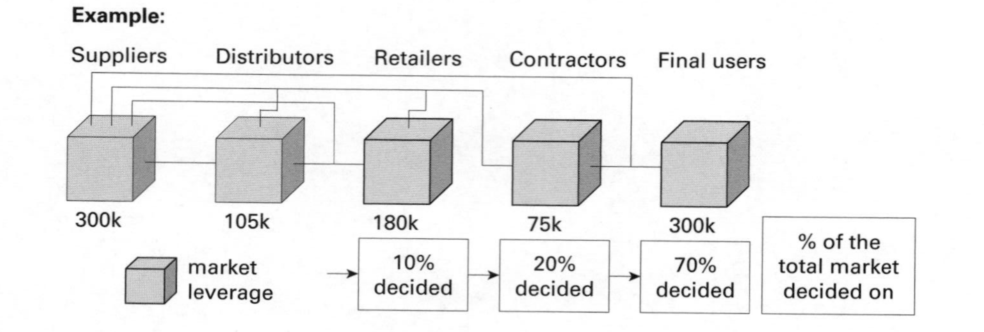

What do our customers want?

06

At the end of this chapter, you will understand:

- That customers never have, and never will be, rational
- How to understand customers' needs and wants (without spending any money!)
- How to harness all your knowledge and wisdom in making a better offer to customers

Introduction

This chapter deals with the third heading in the Strategic Marketing Plan, SWOT analyses, shown below.

The first point to make is about the word 'want' in the title to this chapter. As you saw in Chapter 5, people are not rational in their behaviour, no matter what the economists might say.

Most business people will have read about the Coca Cola/Pepsi taste tests, which have been repeated many times over the past 40 years, always with the same results. In 'blind' tasting, a substantial majority prefer Pepsi. The same people, however, when tasting from bottles with the labels on, prefer Coca Cola by a significant majority.

Customers have never known what they want, so don't ask them!

Even neurologists agree that people are not rational when choosing between products, as can be seen from the reference shown in Figure 6.1.

The contents of a Strategic Marketing Plan (T+3, fewer than 20 pages)

- Financial Summary
- Market Overview
  - how the market works
  - key segments and their needs
- SWOT Analyses of Segments
- Portfolio Summary of SWOTS
- Assumptions
- Objectives and Strategies
- Budget for Three Years

Figure 6.1 Neurology and brand preference

'Ventromedial prefrontal cortex (VMPC) is a critical neural substrate for the effect of Commercial brand information on human decision-making and brand preferences. The key finding of this study provides direct evidence that brand preference is the Product of factors unrelated to the product taste. This effect is not present with patients with VMPC damage and defects in emotional Processing.'

SOURCE: Koenigs, M and Tranes, D (2008) 'Corfronal cortex damage abolishes brand-cured preference', *SCAN* **3**, pp 2–6, Department of Neurology, University of Iowa College of Medicine

Neurologists repeated the Coke/Pepsi challenge a number of times always with the same result, except that people with a damaged brain section that affects the emotional part of decision-making consistently preferred Pepsi Cola even when shown the brand names. Those respondents with normal ventromedial prefrontal cortex neural substrate consistently preferred Coke on being shown the labels.

Two further examples should convince you – the first repeated from Chapter 3 to reinforce the point.

1 One of the big carmakers organized a competitor comparison day, buying one example of every rival model in a particular category

and lining them up in a row. Each car was silver and the badges had been removed. Not only could the assembled experts not tell them apart, they couldn't even pick out their own car!

2 An extreme case has to be level of pseudo-scientific jargon and meaningless polysyllables used in advertising, often seen for products such as skincare, shampoo and the like.

Hence the crucial importance of Chapter 5, for a failure to understand market segmentation, irrespective of whether you are a business-to-business firm or a business-to-consumer firm, will prevent you from making offers that really meet not only their needs, but also their wants.

Don't waste money on bad market research

This heading may seem a little strange coming from a Professor of Marketing. The reality, however, is that most market research about customers and consumers is wasted, largely because we ask inane questions about what they want, to which they invariably give rational answers.

To illustrate this point, let me give you an example. A friend of mine, who prided himself on his rational behaviour, decided to apply a rational process to his new car purchase. He collected the brochures for 20 cars and analysed them on a spreadsheet according to factors such as speed, price, depreciation and so on. Not only did he have a three-tier scoring system, but he also had a weighting system, because he reckoned he was less interested in price than speed, etc. He scored all 20 models, multiplied the score by the weight and ended up with a rank order of cars from 1 to 20.

He subsequently asked my advice, as he was clearly unhappy with the results of his own analysis. I asked him why he didn't want the number one ranked car. His response? 'It's a salesman's car'. His reason for being unhappy with the number two ranked car was 'It's an old man's car'. His reason for being unhappy with the third ranked car was 'It's a boy-racer car'. I eventually asked him which car he really wanted, to which he replied: 'It's really difficult Malcolm, because I quite fancy a BMW'. 'But,' I said, 'you can't have a BMW because it's number 19 on your list.' To which he replied: 'Yes, it's really difficult, isn't it?'

Of course, he eventually bought a BMW, but if someone had asked him stupid questions about why he bought a BMW, the truth about the emotional reasons for his purchase would not have been revealed. Top-rated market research companies use many tried-and-tested research techniques to elicit people's real reasons for buying.

Please try to remember the segmentation example given in Chapter 5 about buyers of IT, repeated here as Figure 6.2.

Figure 6.2 Understand the different category buyers

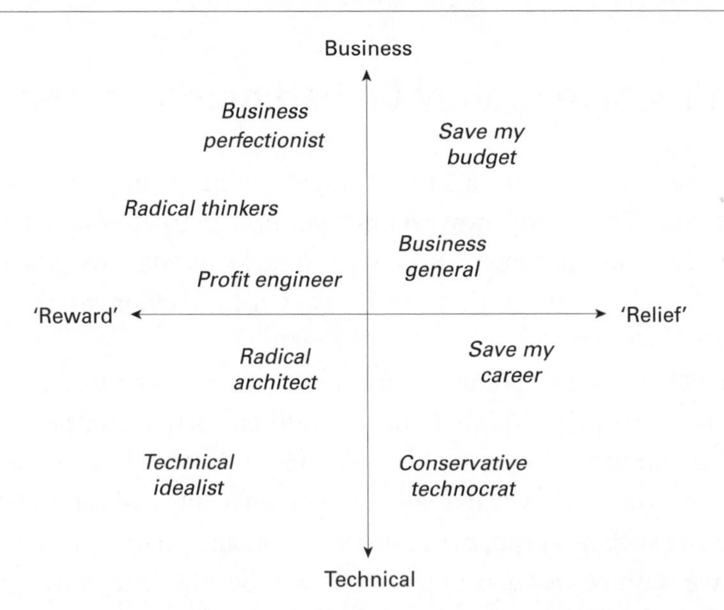

Every market in the world is segmented. All we have to do is find out what these segments are and what they need.

Each of the nine segments shown is different from the others and it is quite easy to imagine how each segment would respond to approaches from suppliers of IT equipment. Let's not forget that it isn't companies that buy things, it is **people** in companies and people don't stop being people just because they are performing a role in a company.

Most companies, however, 'marmalade' their average message across some mythical, average buyer of IT. The result? Because they don't understand the buyer's real motivations, they inevitably end up having to do a deal on price.

Excellent market research organizations, of course, will not waste your money asking silly questions and there are a number of techniques to elicit the truth about customer motivations that do not involve asking questions.

Please don't ask customers what they want.

If you are an SME, for example, there is absolutely no reason why you can't emulate the excellence of the 3Ms, GEs and Proctor & Gambles of the world when it comes to understanding real customer needs. P&G, for example, before launching products in, say, China, spend time living with families to observe actual behaviours so that when they do launch, they always hit the bullseye.

As a hypothetical example, let's take a company whose customers include factory managers. By observing their environment, the noise, the irritations, the blockages, the interruptions, etc, it is then possible to go back to the 'laboratory' and invent something that helps to reduce all these problems.

Let's take one more hypothetical example. Imagine a 19th-century horse and carriage with four passengers. At a stop, one of our early market researchers approaches them and asks them what they want. The first passenger says: 'Could you please go away and invent the internal combustion engine?' 'What's that?' asks the researcher. 'It's the associated corpuscular emissions per zero point zero gram of air, producing ions carrying one electrostatic quantity of electricity of either sign...'

The next passenger says: 'This horse stinks – could you go away and invent air conditioning please?'

You need a process for harnessing all the knowledge and wisdom you already possess.

The next passenger says: 'Could you please go away and invent ABS brakes?'

The fourth passenger says: 'Could you please go away and invent windscreen wipers?'

And so on, after ridiculous so on. As Henry Ford said: 'If I had asked customers what they want, they would have said "A faster horse!"'

Have I made my point by now? Your job is to understand the environment in which your customers work and to come up with solutions (offers) that make their lives easier, more profitable, etc – see Chapter 4 on value propositions.

The best way to understand customer needs is to observe them in their everyday environment.

A process for understanding what customers want (without spending money)

Please don't think I am about to suggest that you should all become sophisticated market researchers. You definitely don't need to employ any consultants, as I am about to show you how you can proceed to do a much better job of understanding your customers' real needs. After all – and this has always been my experience of all companies – you already have a wealth of data, information, knowledge and wisdom about their markets and their customers, otherwise they wouldn't have got as far as they have. All you need is a process for harnessing all this wisdom and this is what follows.

You cannot, however, implement this part of the process if you have yet to complete the market segmentation exercise in Chapter 5, otherwise you will be adding yet more nonsense to this existing nonsense.

SWOTs, not SWAGs

(A SWAG is a scientific, wild-aimed guess!)
Nearly everyone knows what a SWOT is – it is an analysis of strengths, weaknesses, opportunities and threats. My experience, however, of SWOTs is that they are about as useful as an ashtray on a motorbike!

Why is this? Figure 6.3 shows what SWOTs normally look like and you will observe that I have scrawled across the middle of the diagram, the word 'WRONG'.

Figure 6.3 Example of a traditional SWOT diagram

> *Most SWOT analyses are as useless as an ashtray on a motorbike.*

As a veteran presenter at in-company workshops and conferences, I travel all over the world and often visit the business part of the hotel in which I am staying. In every syndicate room, in every hotel in the world, there is a flip chart with a SWOT on it and they ALL say more or less the same things.

Under 'Threats', they all list: 'the weather; competitors; government legislation,' etc. Then on the 'Opportunities' side, they all list: 'the weather; competitors; government legislation' – so note the irony in this totally unproductive method.

Don't use meaningless words in SWOT analyses.

Let me give you some more fatuous examples in Figure 6.4, where words are written down without any thought given to their real meaning.

Figure 6.4 'Motherhood!' Strengths statements

Strengths	Please tick appropriate boxes	Hidden Meanings
High quality		We can't think of any real reason why we do business in this market . . .
Low price		That must explain it . . .
Personal service		We still can't . . .
High value to customers		Our products are a bit expensive, but we still sell some
Old-established firm		We must be OK, we've survived so far
Technologically sophisticated		We know more than the customer
Product strengths		Look at the product, never mind the customer
The 'natural' supplier to this market		We don't know who our competitors are
We are the industry standard		We don't think we have any competition

From my sceptical interpretation of these strengths and weaknesses (with thanks to Professor Nigel Piercy from Swansea University Business School for his original thinking about this topic), you will see that they abuse words and that they come out in a meaningless cacophony.

Even worse, this vapid stream of words reaches a sort of 'my head is in the oven, my feet are in the fridge, so on average I am quite comfortable' conclusion, especially when we apply the technique to any commercial group other than a real segment.

Guidelines for a better approach

Before setting out a more robust way of carrying out a SWOT analysis, let me set out some guidelines to ensure a more meaningful output. These are shown in Figure 6.5.

Figure 6.5 Guidelines for a better SWOT analysis

Strengths	**Weaknesses**
• It can create value for the organization and customers • It is unique • It is inimitable • It is lasting	• It is meaningful to the customer • It is unique • It is difficult to fix
Opportunities • It is large • It is accessible • It is lasting	**Threats** • It is significant • It is lasting

A process and a template for doing a proper SWOT

Conducting a meaningful SWOT, however, is still quite a difficult task that will, alas, consume some of your valuable time. The results, however, will more than compensate for taking your attention away from the pressing day-to-day problems that confront you. My advice is to set aside a morning or afternoon to meet with a small team of colleagues to complete SWOT analyses on at least five or six segments. Include in your team at least one person who is closely involved with customers, either in a sales or customer service capacity, one person who understands the product/service well and one person who understands your database well. If you have a marketing executive, include him or her.

This small team of four or five people should find an environment in which they will not be interrupted and should be prepared to be totally open-minded about the task to be undertaken. Figure 6.6 is the template to be completed; Figure 6.7 is an example. It can be seen from column 1 that the exercise should be completed on a *segment* hence, if you have discovered six or seven segments from your work resulting from Chapter 5, you will need to do six or seven SWOT analyses.

Set aside time for conducting proper SWOT analyses on segments.

The following three figures explain the process. Figure 6.8 is the template to complete for each segment.

Step-by-step process for an effective SWOT analysis

1. Identify the Critical Success Factors (CSFs) that influence the customers' decision. There are usually not more than six really important factors.
2. Assign an importance weighting to each CSF so that the weightings for each segment totals 100 per cent.
3. Identify the key competitors for each segment and score performance of your company and each key competitor on a scale of 1 to 10, where 1 = very poor and 10 = excellent. Limit to a few competitors (between 1 and 3).
4. Multiply the weights by the scores and add up the weighted score for each competitor.
5. Assess your relative strength by dividing your score by the best competitor's score.
6. Identify the key issues from the analysis.
7. Note that you can change you relative business strength by focusing on improving your strength on the criteria that matter most to customers.

Involve a multi-disciplinary team in completing SWOT analyses.

Figure 6.6 Effective template for completing a SWOT analysis

Product-market: ____________________________

CSFs	Weights	Score/weighting Above the diagonal line: Score out of 10 Below the diagonal line: Multiply score x weight			
		You	Compet A	Compet B	Compet C
1.					
2.					
3.					
4.					
5.					
6.					
Totals	100				

Relative Business Strength: ____ (Our score minus best competitor score)

Figure 6.7 Example for how to complete SWOT analysis template (Critical Success Factors)

CSFs	Weights	Score/weight Score out of 10 - multiplying these by the weight			
		You	Compet A	Compet B	Compet C
1. Thought leadership	50	6 / 3.0	8 / 4.0		
2. Impact on practice throughout	25	8 / 2.0	7 / 1.8		
3. Patient satisfaction	15	7 / 1.1	10 / 1.5		
4. Impact on practice budget	10	6 / 0.6	5 / 0.5		
5.					
6.					
Totals	100	6.7	7.8		

Relative Business Strength: –1.1

Figure 6.8 Strategic marketing planning exercise – SWOT analysis

1. SEGMENT DESCRIPTION
It should be a *specific* part of the business and should be *very important* to the organization.

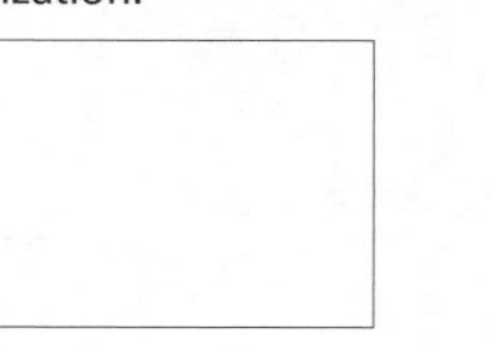

2. CRITICAL SUCCESS FACTORS
In other words, how do customers choose?

1	
2	
3	
4	
5	

3. WEIGHTING
How important is each of these CSFs? Score out of 100.

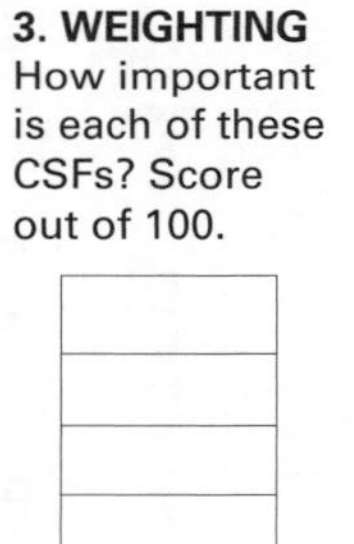

Total 100

4. STRENGTHS/WEAKNESSES ANALYSIS
How would your customers score you and each of your main competitors out of 10 on each of the CSFs? Multiply the score by the weight.

	You	Comp A	Comp B	Comp C	Comp D
1					
2					
3					
4					
5					
°					

5. OPPORTUNITIES/THREATS
What are the few things outside your direct control that have had, and will have, an impact on this part of your business?

OPPORTUNITIES

1	
2	
3	
4	
5	

THREATS

6. KEY ISSUES THAT NEED TO BE ADDRESSED
What are the really key issues from the SWOT that need to be addressed?

In box 2 (Critical Success Factors – CSFs) of Figure 6.8, it can be seen that there are only five spaces. The problem here, however, is that there is a tendency to write down words such as 'Product Performance', 'Price', 'Service', etc, all of which are meaningless unless accompanied by a more detailed explanation.

Ensure that 'critical success factor' analysis is properly understood.

The following simple case will explain a methodology for making the summary of CSFs more meaningful.

In 2008, the recession led to a decline in the number of parents sending their children to independent/private schools. In other words, sales declined for most independent schools. The knee-jerk reaction of independent schools was to drop the price, with the inevitable result that the whole sector became unprofitable.

Faced with this dilemma, my company was asked to help. Figure 6.9 shows the five key buying factors that parents took account of when considering which school to send their child to. It is important to stress that uncovering these key buying factors did NOT require research, as the schools already knew them – it was just that until then no one had asked them to rationalize what they already knew!

Figure 6.9 Five critical success factors for independent schools

1. Academic
2. School/family relationships
3. Convenience
4. Costs
5. Enhancement

It was a simple task after that to explore in more detail what each heading really meant and some of the details for just one of these headings are shown in Figure 6.10. The same level of detail was generated for each of the four other factors. Just understand how easy it was to generate these details from the heads of these very experienced people.

Executives in the independent school sector already knew the factors for success. All that was required was a process to elicit this knowledge from them.

The next step was obviously to generate a number of segments of parents, for clearly not all parents have the same needs or considerations in choosing an independent school for their child.

Figure 6.10 Academic success factors for independent schools

1. Personality and vision of Head
2. Exam results
3. Class size
4. League table position (compared with regional competitors)
5. Student academic successes (Oxbridge, major universities, competitions)
6. Academic planning: A level, IB, pre-U; GCSE? New subjects?
7. Quality/knowledge/experience of staff
8. Facilities for teaching and learning
9. Learning opportunities outside mainstream subjects (could be vocational skills)
10. Reporting procedures
11. Innovations in teaching and learning

The main point, however, is that it is all right to write in Figure 6.8 box 2, for example, 'Academic factors', because behind this there will be a deep understanding of what this really means in the case of a particular segment.

Independent schools are, of course, SMEs, so let's not forget the relevance of this example.

More importantly, however, is the fact that, having done this SWOT analysis on each segment, each independent school can now look at its asset base and appeal, via communications, to those segments to which it is most likely to appeal.

The main points to take from this little case example are:

- Irrespective of the 2008 recession, these schools had absolutely no reason to reduce their prices. All they needed to do was to harness the knowledge and wisdom they already possessed, using the processes outlined in Chapter 5 and in this chapter.

- Zero market research was involved, as the independent schools already knew this stuff.
- They could now carry out focused, meaningful SWOTs on each segment.

Let's now move to box 3 in Figure 6.8. This requires each CSF to be weighted according to its relevance/importance of each segment. Usually, once the hard work has been done in box 2, this isn't too difficult to fathom, but if it is important and if you have real doubts, go and talk to some customers. In some cases, it might even be necessary to do some market research, but this should be a last resort.

Having completed a SWOT on each segment, it is now possible to select those that most closely match our asset base.

In the above case of independent schools, one segment might rank certain aspects of academic achievement very highly, with price being of lesser importance.

Once this step has been completed, it is possible to move to the fourth box in Figure 6.8. Make a note your own organization's score out of 10 for each CSF as well as the score for at least one major competitor. A simple process then follows of multiplying the scores by the weights to arrive at a weighted score out of 100 or 1,000 for you and at least one major competitor.

These weighted scores will indicate why you are the best competitor in this segment or – if not, where your weaknesses lie compared with your competitors.

This step is crucial in developing a winning strategy to grow sales and profits, because these weighted scores will later become the driver of your strategies to achieve your objectives. This will form the basis of Chapter 8.

Remember the chapter on value propositions? The results from your SWOT analyses will also form the basis of your value propositions.

This process will clearly establish what you need to improve to succeed in each segment.

Box 5 in Figure 6.8 features the opportunities and threats from outside the company as they related to each segment. They are NOT internal and at this stage are NOT things you will do. The final step in completing a SWOT analysis for each segment is to summarize all the key issues arising from your analysis (box 6).

The lessons to be learned from the independent schools case are crucial to conducting truly powerful SWOT analyses on each important product/market segment.

I must stress here once again that a SWOT should be conducted on ALL segments, of which there are likely to be at least seven or eight. So it can be seen that this is the most time-consuming and most difficult of all the strategy-formulation steps. Done correctly and diligently, the setting of objectives and strategies becomes a lot easier and more productive.

Opportunities and threats are outside your control.

Figure 6.11 A summary of the process described above

- Critical Success Factors provide a customer-focused way of assessing the strengths and weaknesses of our offering.
- Obtain a customer view where possible – otherwise use a team of those who are close to the customer.
- Validate the results against current financials.
- Our weighted average score, compared with the best competitor score is plotted on the horizontal axis of the Directional Policy Matrix.
- Focus on real segments, not on the whole market.
- Shared vision – it works best if done in a small, experienced group.
- Expressions like 'customer orientation' are meaningless.It is only meaningful if explained properly and if customers really value it.
- Opportunities and threats exist outside the organization – they are not things we plan to do.

Finally...

Often it is forgotten that in conducting SWOT analyses, we have had to make assumptions, or educated guesses about some of the factors that will affect our business, for example: about market growth rates; about government economic policies; about the activities of our competitors, etc. So, all that is necessary now before proceeding to the next crucial step, is to list your important assumptions. Examples of assumptions might be:

'With respect to the company's industrial climate, it is assumed that:

- Industrial over-capacity will increase from 105 per cent to 110 per cent as new plants come into operation.
- Price competition will force price levels down by 5 per cent across the board.'

Assumptions should be few in number and if your plans are possible irrespective of the assumptions made, then the assumptions are unnecessary...

We are now ready to proceed to the next step – setting our objectives and strategies.

Actions

1 Complete a SWOT analysis for each segment identified in Chapter 5 using the analysis sheet shown in Figure 6.12.

2 Make assumptions for each segment.

Figure 6.12 Strategic marketing planning exercise – SWOT analysis

1. SEGMENT DESCRIPTION
It should be a *specific* part of the business and should be *very important* to the organization.

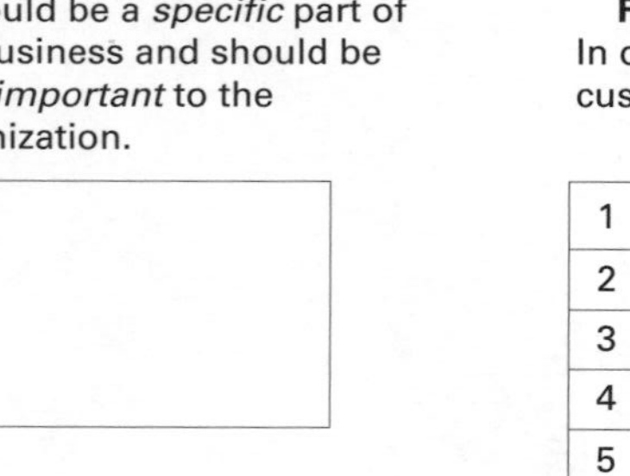

2. CRITICAL SUCCESS FACTORS
In other words, how do customers choose?

1	
2	
3	
4	
5	

3. WEIGHTING
How important is each of these CSFs? Score out of 100.

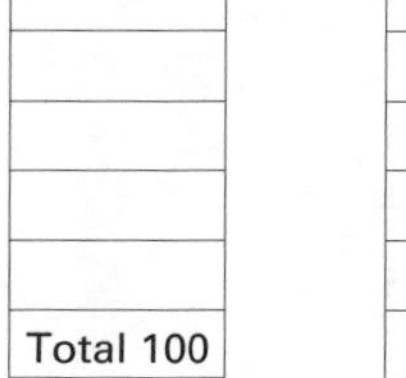

Total 100

4. STRENGTHS/WEAKNESSES ANALYSIS
How would your customers score you and each of your main competitors out of 10 on each of the CSFs? Multiply the score by the weight.

	You	Comp A	Comp B	Comp C	Comp D
1					
2					
3					
4					
5					
°					

5. OPPORTUNITIES/THREATS
What are the few things outside your direct control that have had, and will have, an impact on this part of your business?

OPPORTUNITIES

1	
2	
3	
4	
5	

THREATS

6. KEY ISSUES THAT NEED TO BE ADDRESSED
What are the really key issues from the SWOT that need to be addressed?

How to set marketing objectives

07

By the end of this chapter, you will be able to:

- Select which segments to focus your resources on
- Set qualified objectives for the selected segments

Introduction

The first thing to point out is that the heading of this chapter is 'How to set *marketing* objectives'. The reason for this, you may recall from Chapter 1, is because all the best companies set their objectives and strategies for what to sell and to whom *before* allocating resources to Research and Development, Production, Distribution and the like. Obviously in setting these marketing objectives and strategies, they have to be tentative initially and it is crucial to check with other functions that the necessary resources, including finance, to achieve these objectives are available. But, once these sensible checks are made, the marketing objectives and strategies can be firmed up, the strategic marketing plan can be finalized and then you can proceed to prepare all other functional plans.

*Marketing objectives and strategies should be set **before** all other functional objectives and strategies.*

As a reminder, please see Table 7.1 repeated from Chapter 2.

Table 7.1 Corporate objectives and strategies

- Objective (what):
  - Profit
- Strategies (how):
  - facilities (operations, R&D, IT, distribution, etc)
  - people (personnel)
  - money (finance)
  - products and markets (marketing)
  - other (CSR, image, etc)

Also, please look at this Strategic Marketing Plan box once more, as we are about to complete the 'Portfolio Summary of SWOTs' prior to setting marketing objectives and strategies.

The contents of a Strategic Marketing Plan (T+3, fewer than 20 pages)

- Financial Summary
- Market Overview
  - how the market works
  - key segments and their needs
- SWOT Analyses of Segments
- Portfolio Summary of SWOTS
- Assumptions
- Objectives and Strategies
- Budget for Three Years

*Any objective **must** be quantified.*

What are marketing objectives?

Setting marketing objectives and strategies is the key step in the whole process of developing a plan to grow sales and profits. An objective is what you want to achieve. Strategies are how you intend to achieve your objective.

There can be objectives and strategies at all corporate levels. For example, there are corporate objectives and strategies marketing objectives and strategies, distribution objectives and strategies, advertising objectives and strategies, pricing objectives and strategies and so on. Any objective, however, must be **quantified**, otherwise it is not an objective, so words like 'reduce', 'improve', 'increase', etc are not acceptable.

Marketing objectives are about products and markets only.

Common sense will confirm that it is only by selling something to someone that the company's financial goals can be achieved, so this forms the basis of marketing objectives, which are about products and markets only. In essence, marketing objectives are simply about one or more of the following:

- existing products in existing markets;
- new products for existing markets;
- existing products for new markets;
- new products for new markets.

These, of course, are derived from the Ansoff Matrix, already discussed in Chapter 4 and shown again in Figure 7.1.

Figure 7.1 Ansoff Matrix

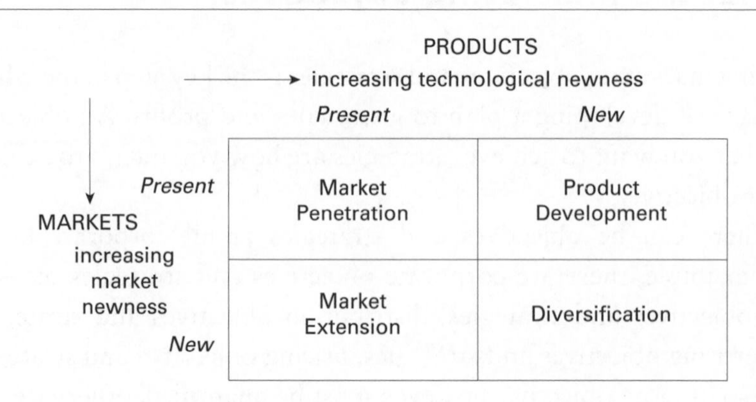

In each of these categories, the only possible objectives are:

- sales revenue;
- sales volume;
- market share;
- penetration – for example, getting a product into 50 per cent of available channels;
- profit (however defined).

Marketing strategies to achieve these objectives will be dealt with in Chapter 8.

Always start your planning from the base of your current products in your current markets.

Because, by definition, all of us live and work in the first box of the Ansoff Matrix, (that is, we have our existing products that we sell in our existing markets), I am going to concentrate on how to set objectives for these, because if we can achieve our MUST objective with our existing products in our existing markets, it will not be necessary to get involved in the more risky options that require us to do new things. I will, however, cover these options in the last chapter because if you can't reach your objectives by doing more of what you are doing now, you will be forced to consider doing other things.

May I please remind you to refer to the rough and appropriate work you did on gap analysis at the end of Chapter 4, as this will guide your thinking in terms of setting objectives and strategies. Remember, however, you must always start planning from the base of your current products in your current markets.

The most useful managerial tool in my experience is the Strategic Planning Matrix.

How to allocate your resources effectively

There is a relatively sophisticated methodology for assessing your current products in their current markets prior to setting appropriate objectives and strategies. It is technically known as The Directional Policy Matrix and in my experience, it is the most useful tool I have ever come across in my long management career.

It is quite sophisticated and technically difficult to construct accurately, so I have developed a simpler version that works just as well and effectively in all environments, including SME. I call this SME version 'The Strategic Planning Matrix' (SPM). There are four boxes in this matrix and it has two very important axes, one of which, the vertical axis, is labelled 'Market Attractiveness'. The horizontal axis is labelled 'Our Relative Competitive Strengths'. A blank SPM looks as shown in Figure 7.2.

Figure 7.2 Strategic Planning Matrix

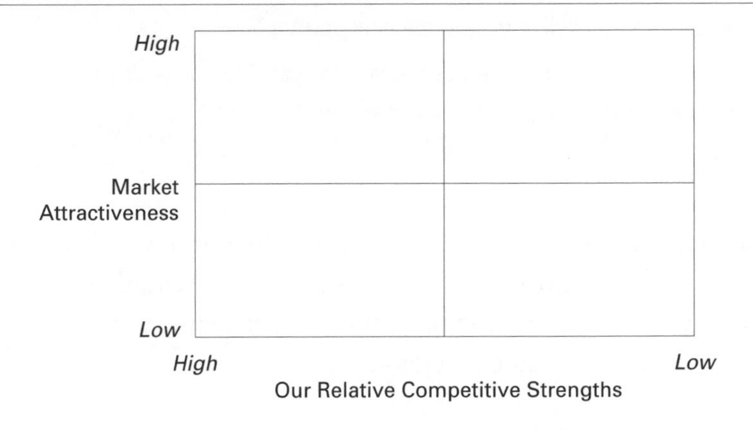

Please note that on the horizontal axis 'high' is on the left and 'low' is on the right. This is because most executives will be familiar with the Boston Matrix, in which 'high' was at the point of origin. Also, another famous management guru, Michael Porter, put 'high' on the left of his matrices.

What should be plotted on the Strategic Planning Matrix (SPM)?

For the purpose of this crucial chapter, I am going to assume that you did at least some elementary thinking about market segments (from Chapter 5) and that you identified at least three or four in each of your main markets.

However, let us look again at Table 7.2, repeated from Chapter 4. As a minimum, select the principal boxes from Table 7.2, so you may select, for example, six or seven boxes that account for at least 80 per cent of your sales. These will be your 'markets' for the vertical axis of the SPM.

1. Select a business unit, or part of the business, for which you wish to develop a partial plan. Business unit: ____________________
2. Along the top of the table below, list the principal products, product groups or services sold by the business unit, ignoring unimportant ones.
3. Down the left of the table, list the principal markets, or market segments, you sell into, ignoring unimportant ones.
4. Now choose four to six product-markets (cells) to concentrate on. For each, estimate your current revenue in the box.

If you only have one main product (or product group) into one main market, or even into two main markets, it is essential that you go back to Chapter 5 and complete the market segmentation exercise, even if it is only the 'quick' version.

Table 7.2 Product–market table

Products: Markets:	1:	2:	3:	4:	5:	6:	7:
1:							
2:							
3:							
4:							
5:							
6:							
7:							

If you are competing in a market in which there are only a few major customers (Key Accounts), as in the case of the car industry, or the supermarket sector in the UK, list these customers for positioning on the vertical axis of the SPM. These customers will be the equivalent of 'markets'.

To summarize, make a list here of Markets, Segments, or Key Accounts.

We are going to use current products in current markets as the unit of analysis for completing the SPM. Ideally, these should be segments.

What does 'Market Attractiveness' mean?

As I said above, the vertical axis of the SPM, labelled 'Market Attractiveness', is the most important of the two axes, because it will determine how you allocate your scarce resources. The real significant definition of 'Market Attractiveness' is 'The potential for growing profits over the next three years', as profit growth is what we are interested in. Whilst it is possible to make an assessment intuitively of which of the seven or eight markets we have listed above offers the best opportunities for profit growth, there is a more robust and 'scientific' way of doing this, which I will now explain.

Profit is the sum of market size, profit margin and potential growth.

Profit, of course, is the sum of market size (revenue), multiplied by potential growth (%), multiplied by return on sales (%). We are interest in the **future** (that is, prospects for the next three years) and the data you use should be realistic and should apply equally to **all** competitors in these markets. In other words, return on sales should be the weighted average of the margin that is available to **any** competitor in a market.

As an example, if a market is worth £100 million and is growing at 10 per cent a year at an ROS of 10 per cent, over three years, the profit potential for all competitors would be:

$100 \times 10 = 10$ million

$110 \times 10 = 11$ million

$121 \times 10 = 12.1$ million

$133 \times 10 = 13.3$ million

46.4 million

There is, however, no need to do such calculations, as the method explained in the next few paragraphs will make clear.

Figure 7.3 Market Attractiveness Factors (MAFs) Process

1. At the corporate level, decide what the MAFs are (usually three to five factors).
2. Give each MAF an importance weighting to the company (total weights should sum to 100 per cent).
3. For each MAF, define the scoring criteria (what constitutes low attractiveness, medium attractiveness, and high attractiveness).
4. Using the scoring criteria, score each product-market on a scale of 0 to 10 against each factor (where 0 is extremely low and 10 is extremely high attractiveness).
5. Multiply the importance weights by the attractiveness scores to produce a weighted attractiveness score.
6. Evaluate the total weighted scores – do they seem to make sense, intuitively?

Figure 7.3 describes the process of setting Market Attractiveness Factors (MAFs) and Figure 7.4 is a completed example for one market. This calculation, of course, will need to be carried out for all your markets in order to establish the relative attractiveness of each. A form for this is provided in Table 7.4. Although in this table there are four MAFs, it is perfectly acceptable to use only the first three.

Looking at Table 7.4, you will see that your first task is to set the parameters for each of the MAFs. For a very small company, an attractive market size might be £1 million, whereas for a bigger company it might be £10 million. An attractive ROS might be 25 per cent for one company and 15 per cent for another. You will see that the next task is to assign a weight for each MAF. This is an important step, because it depends on your circumstances; for example, if you have a factory with, say, only 40 per cent occupancy, you would give a bigger weight to size and growth. On the other hand, if you have a factory that is full to capacity, you would give a bigger weight to profitability. So this step is very important and you should give careful thought to it. Once you have done this, you can then use Table 7.5 to carry out your calculations.

Table 7.3 Example of Market Attractiveness evaluation for one market only

Factor	Scoring Criteria			Score	Weighting	Ranking
	10–7	6–4	3–0			
1. Market Size (£ millions)	> £250	£51–250	< £50	5	15	0.75
2. Volume Growth (Units)	> 10%	5–9%	< 5%	10	40	4.0
3. Industry Profitability	> 15%	10–15%	< 10%	8	35	2.8
4. Competitive Intensity	Low	Medium	High	6	10	0.6
					Total	**8.15**

This form illustrates a quantitative approach to evaluating market attractiveness. Each factor is scored, then multiplied by the percentage weighting and added up for the overall score. In this example, an overall score of 8.15 out of 10 places this market in the highly attractive category. It is necessary to calculate the relative attractiveness of ALL your markets using this method.

Table 7.4 Market Attractiveness evaluation

Factor (amend)	Scoring Criteria (amend)			Weighting (amend)	Ranking (amend)
	10–7	6–4	3–0		
1. Market Size (£ millions)	> £250	£51–250	< £50	15	0.75
2. Volume Growth (Units)	> 10%	5–9%	< 5%	40	4.0
3. Industry Profitability	> 15%	10–15%	< 10%	35	2.8
4. Competitive Intensity	Low	Medium	High	10	0.6
				Total	**8.15**

This form illustrates a quantitative approach to evaluating market attractiveness. Each factor is scored, then multiplied by the percentage weighting and totalled for the overall score. In this example, an overall score of 8.15 out of 10 places this market in the highly attractive category. Decide on MAFs. Decide on the parameters. Decide on the weighting. Put ALL your markets/segments through this process.

Table 7.5 Market Attractiveness Factors

Attractiveness	Weight (%)	Product-market:		Product-market:		Product-market:	
		Score	Score x weight	Score	Score x weight	Score	Score x weight
Total	100%						

Please pay close attention to the weights you allocate to the MAFs.

All you have to do now is to take your markets (from Table 7.2) or your segments (identified from Chapter 5), score each one out of 10, then multiply the score by the weight to arrive at a weighted score, as in the example given in Table 7.3. You can use the proforma given in Table 7.5 for this purpose.

I am sorry about this, dear reader, but you are going to have to do this for every one of your 'markets', so it will take up a bit of your time – but it will be worth the effort – trust me! Copy the form in Table 7.5 for this purpose.

When you have done this, place each of your 'markets' on a thermometer, as shown below in Figure 7.4.

Figure 7.4 Market Attractiveness thermometer

The following is a very useful tip in completing this exercise, so please read this next section.

My experience over many years of doing this exercise with companies is that most of the weighted scores range from 3.5 for the lowest and 7.5 for the highest. For reasons that will be clear later, in this case you should start the scale on the bottom of the axis at 3.0 and the top at 8.0 so that there is a proper spread of your markets, otherwise, if you make this scale 1–10, they will all cluster around the middle of the vertical axis. As you will appreciate later, this makes this particular analysis virtually useless.

It is also important that you get a wide spread of your markets on the horizontal axis.

What does 'Our Relative Competitive Strength' mean on the horizontal axis?

This book is written for successful companies who want to be even more successful, so by now you will already have worked out for yourselves that this is the easy part of this analysis for the Strategic Planning Matrix (SPM), because you have already done a SWOT analysis for each of your markets.

So, all you have to do now is to put the weighted score from your SWOTs for each of your markets on the horizontal axis, using the same 'rule' I explained for the vertical axis.

In other words, if your lowest weighted SWOT score was, say 3.5 and your highest was, say 7.5, make the point of origin on the horizontal an 8.0 and 3.0 on the right.

This will ensure that you have a wide spread of your markets when you complete this exercise. You will soon see why this is important.

How to complete this Strategic Planning Matrix

All you have to do now is to find the coordinates from both axes, initially as dots.

Now draw a circle reflecting either:

- the market size of each market, or;
- your sales into each of these markets.

Ideally, do both, with your sales (a smaller circle) inside the larger one (market size) in order to appreciate your relative position in each. It is all right, however, if you just make the circle size represent your own sales.

It is important that you get a wide spread of your markets on the vertical axis.

So, let's assume that you have drawn only circles representing, proportionally, your sales into each market. Consequently, the circles should add up to about 100 per cent of your current sales. You should end up with an SPM that looks something like the matrix in Figure 7.5.

Figure 7.5 Selecting and categorizing markets by potential

Our Relative Competitive Strengths

Market Attractiveness	High	Low
High	Strategic investment Strategic	Selective investment Star
Low	Proactive maintenance Status	Management for cash Streamline

Each box in the Strategic Planning Matrix requires different objectives and strategies.

How to interpret your SPM

In the example in Figure 7.5, there are 11 markets shown, each circle representing the supplier's sales value in each market rather than each circle representing the available potential.

Box 1 – bottom left – shows markets where the supplier has excellent strengths, but for reasons known to the supplier, these markets do not offer much potential for growth in their profits over the next three years. This being the case, the supplier should keep the cash flows coming as long as possible, only investing when necessary in order to keep the business coming in. Net free cash flows from these markets are what keeps the company going. You will see that I have labelled these markets 'Status'.

Markets in box 2 in the bottom right of the SPM are neither attractive, nor do we have relative strengths. Clearly, in these markets we should endeavour to minimize costs and squeeze as much net free cash flow as possible from them. I have labelled these markets 'Streamline'.

Markets in box 3, top right, are attractive to us, but we lack competitive strengths. The decision we have to make here is whether to invest in improving our competitive position or whether to just accept this. If we decide to invest in order to improve our competitiveness, under no circumstances should you set inappropriate objectives such as to maximize profitability. This would be a bit like putting a plant in the garden, expecting it to blossom in the spring, whilst pulling it up by the roots every day to see if it is growing! I have labelled these markets 'Star'.

Finally, markets in box 4, top left, represent our real future, for not only do they have great potential for us to grow our profits over the next three years, but we also have relative competitive strengths. I have labelled these markets 'Strategic'.

These guidelines are summarized in the SPM shown in Figure 7.6. Expanded guidelines are shown in Figure 7.7. Please read these guidelines carefully before thinking about setting objectives for the markets in your SPM.

Figure 7.6 Supplier business strength with segment

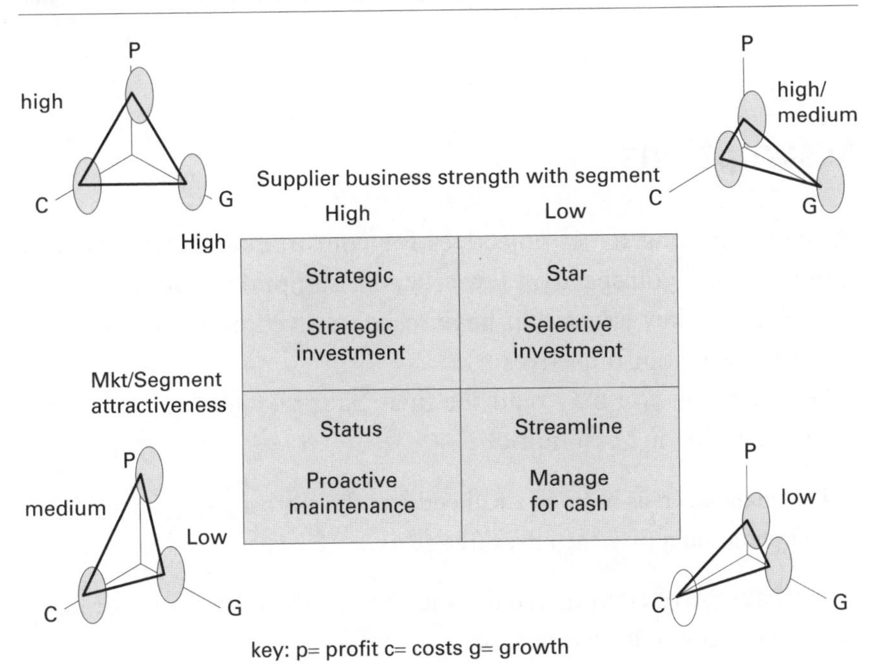

Figure 7.7 Objectives and strategies suggested by portfolio matrix analysis

MARKET SEGMENT ATTRACTIVENESS	Higher (RELATIVE BUSINESS STRENGTH)	Lower (RELATIVE BUSINESS STRENGTH)
Higher	INVEST FOR GROWTH: • Gain/Defend leadership • Accept moderate short-term profits and negative cash flow • Geographic expansion, product line expansion, product differentiation • Aggressive marketing posture – selling, advertising, pricing, sales promotion, service levels, etc	OPPORTUNISTIC: • Move to left if resources are available • Keep a low profile until resources are available • Divest to a buyer able to exploit the opportunity
Lower	MAINTAIN/MANAGE FOR SUSTAINED EARNINGS: • Manage key product lines, prune less successful product lines • Differentiate products to maintain share • Limit marketing expenditure • Stabilize prices except where a temporary aggressive stance is needed	SELECTIVE/MANAGE FOR PROFIT & CASH: • Acknowledge low growth • Identify/exploit growth segments • Emphasize quality, avoid commodity • Improve productivity • Prune product line aggressively, maximize cash flow, minimize marketing expenditure, maintain or raise prices at expense of volume

Assumptions

Before proceeding to set objectives for your markets/segments, it is important that you specify a few crucial assumptions. These are usually related to key issues that have to be resolved or achieved if you are to achieve your objectives.

For example, you may read the financial press very carefully and make the following assumption:

> The financial crisis in France will end and the market will grow by 5 per cent per annum over the next three years.

Or perhaps there is an internal issue that needs to be resolved, leading to the following assumption:

We will be able to recruit five graduates with the essential Information Systems skills that we need.

However, please be sure to make your assumptions few in number and if you can achieve an objective even if your assumption doesn't happen, the assumption is unnecessary.

We can now set objectives for each market in the SPM

Figure 7.8 shows the circles (markets) as they are and where we want them to be (objectives) in three years' time. Some are bigger, some are smaller and some remain the same size. The aggregation of the circles in three years' time should reach our MUST objectives in terms of revenue, but please note that until we have also set the strategies for achieving these revenue objectives, we will not know whether we will be able to achieve the MUST profit objectives.

I will explain how the circles move either to the left or to the right in Chapter 8, as it is the **strategies** that will make them move.

Figure 7.8 The Strategic Planning Matrix (SPM)

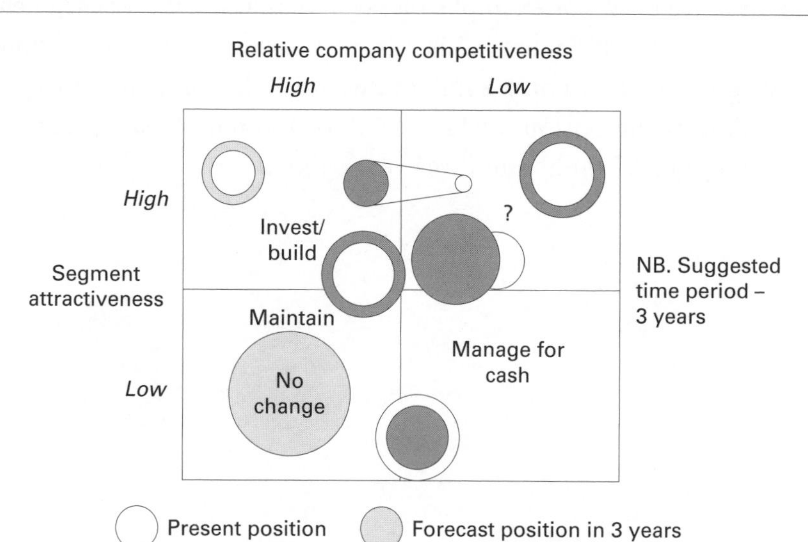

Assumptions should be few in number and if you can achieve your objectives without them, they are unnecessary.

For now, when you have drawn your SPM, the sum of all the circles (markets/segments/customers) should reach your MUST revenue objectives for the next three years. If they don't, you will need to consider either new products for existing markets, or existing products into new markets, or new products into new markets, but this will be dealt with in Chapter 8, alongside spelling out your strategies for achieving your objectives.

For now, however, let's assume that the size of the circles does indeed add up to our MUST revenue objectives in three years' time.

In the next chapter, we can proceed to determine the marketing strategies to achieve the objectives.

Actions

Please display your SPM showing the circles (markets) where they are now and where they will be in three years' time and list the revenue objective for each market, bearing in mind that some might be less than they are now. For example, please note that the market/segment in the middle/top in Figure 7.5 is, say, £5 million in three years' time, growing from its current £1 million, whereas the market/segment in the middle at the bottom of Figure 7.5 is declining from its current £10 million to £7 million in three years' time.

How to set marketing strategies

08

By the end of this chapter, you will be able to:

- Understand the process of new product development
- Understand competitive strategies
- Set strategies to achieve your objectives

Introduction

You will recall that, so far, I have assumed that you can reach your 'MUST' objectives by operating in the first box of the Ansoff Matrix, repeated in Figure 8.1. If, however, you need either new products for existing markets, existing products for new markets, or even new products for new markets, you will need to consider how best to proceed, so this next short section explains a way forward.

Figure 8.1 Ansoff Matrix

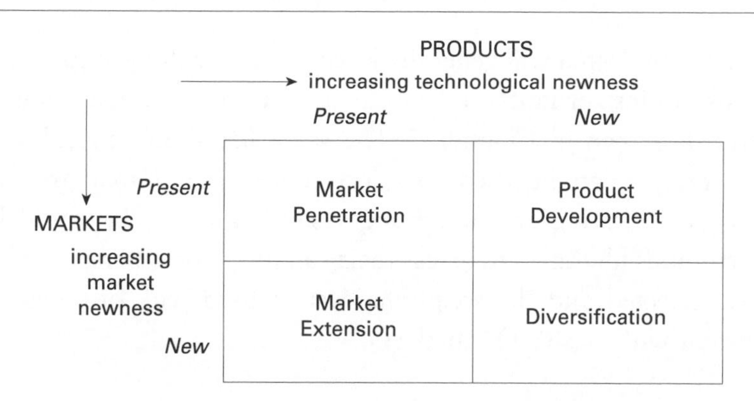

New product development/market extension/diversification

Sooner or later all organizations will need to move along one or both axes of the Ansoff Matrix. How to do this should be comparatively straightforward if the simple guidelines below are followed.

It is not the purpose here to explore in detail subsets of marketing, such as market research, market selection, new product development and diversification. What is important, however, in a book on developing a winning strategy for SMEs, is to communicate an understanding of the framework in which these activities should take place.

What we are aiming to do is to maximize *synergy*, which could be described as the 2 + 2 = 5 effect. The starting point once again is SWOTs (strengths, weaknesses, opportunities and threats). This is so that development of any kind will be firmly based on your company's basic *strengths* and *weaknesses*. External factors are the opportunities and threats facing your company.

Once this important analytical stage is successfully completed, the more technical process of opportunity identification, screening, business analysis and, finally, activities such as product development, testing and entry planning can take place, depending on which option is selected.

The important point to remember is that no matter how thoroughly these subsequent activities are carried out, unless the objectives of product development/market extension are based firmly on an analysis of the company's capabilities, they are unlikely to be successful in the long term.

The criteria selected will generally be consistent with the criteria used for positioning products or businesses in the Strategic Planning Matrix described in Chapter 7. The same list shown in Table 7.5 in Chapter 7 can be used to select those criteria that are most important. A rating and weighting system can then be applied to opportunities identified to assess their suitability or otherwise. Those criteria selected and the weighting system used will, of course, be consistent with the SWOT analyses.

Having said that it is not the purpose of this book to explore in detail any of the subsets of marketing such as market research, it would nonetheless be quite useful briefly to outline the process of new product development and its relationship to the gap analysis that you completed in Chapter 3.

New product development can usefully be seen as a process consisting of the following seven steps:

1. *Idea generation* – the search for product ideas to meet company objectives.
2. *Screening* – a quick analysis of the ideas to establish those that are relevant.
3. *Concept testing* – checking with the market that the new product ideas are acceptable.
4. *Business analysis* – the idea is examined in detail in terms of its commercial fit in the business.
5. *Product development* – making the idea 'tangible'.
6. *Testing* – market tests necessary to verify early business assessments.
7. *Commercialization* – full-scale product launch, committing the company's reputation and resources.

Marketing strategies

In Chapter 7, we set objectives for each of our products for markets. Now we are going to look at strategies for achieving these objectives.

What a company wants to accomplish, in terms of such things as market share and volume, is a marketing objective. How the company intends to go about achieving its objectives is strategy. Strategy is the overall route to the achievement of specific objectives and should describe the means by which objectives are to be reached, the time programme and the allocation of resources. It does not delineate the individual courses the resulting activity will follow.

There is a clear distinction between strategy, and detailed implementation, or tactics.

Strategy is the route to achievement of specific objectives and describes how objectives will be reached.

Marketing strategy reflects the company's best opinion as to how it can most profitably apply its skills and resources to the marketplace. It is inevitably broad in scope.

The plan that stems from it will spell out action and timings and will contain the detailed contribution expected from each.

Marketing strategies are the means by which a company achieves its marketing objectives and are usually concerned with the four Ps: product, price, place and promotion.

There is a similarity between strategy in business and military strategy. One looks at the enemy, the terrain, the resources under command, and then decides whether to attack the whole front, an area of enemy weakness, to feint in one direction whilst attacking in another, or to attempt an encirclement of the enemy's position. The policy and mix, the general direction in which to go, and the criteria for judging success, all come under the heading of strategy. The action steps are tactics.

Similarly, in marketing, the same commitment, mix and type of resources as well as guidelines and criteria that must be met, all come under the heading of strategy.

For example, the decision to use distributors in all but the three largest market areas, in which company salespeople will be used, is a strategic decision. The selection of particular distributors is a tactical decision.

Thus, marketing strategies are the means by which marketing objectives will be achieved and are generally concerned with the four major elements of the marketing mix (the four Ps).

The following headings indicate the general content of strategy statements in the area of marketing:

1 Policies and procedures relating to the products to be offered, such as number, quality, design, branding, packaging, positioning and labelling, etc (product strategies).

2 Pricing levels to be adopted, margins and discount policies (pricing strategies).
3 Advertising, sales promotion, direct mail, call centres and the internet. The mix of these, the creative approach, the type of media, type of displays, the amount to spend, etc (promotion strategies).
4 What emphasis is to be placed on personal selling, the sales approach, sales training, etc (promotion strategies).
5 The distributive channels to be used and the relative importance of each (place strategies).
6 Service levels, etc in relation to different segments.

The following list of marketing strategies (in summary form), covers the majority of options open under the headings of the four Ps:

1 *Product*
   - expand the line;
   - change performance, quality or features;
   - consolidate the line;
   - standardize design;
   - positioning;
   - change the mix;
   - branding.
2 *Price*
   - change price, terms or conditions;
   - skimming policies;
   - penetration policies.
3 *Promotion*
   - change advertising or promotion;
   - change the mix between direct mail, call centres, the internet;
   - change selling.
4 *Place*
   - change delivery or distribution;
   - change service;
   - change channels;
   - change the degree of forward or backward integration.

These two options, that is, terrain or impregnable fortress (or both), are in fact the same options that face businesspeople as they contemplate competitive strategy.

Competitive strategies and how to beat bigger competitors

At this point, let me interrupt the flow of this chapter to tell you a story to illustrate what I suspect you already know – how to beat your competitors.

Imagine three tribes on a small island fighting each other because resources are scarce. One tribe decides to move to a larger adjacent island, sets up camp, and is followed eventually by the other two, who also set up their own separate camps. At first it is a struggle to establish themselves, but eventually they begin to occupy increasing parts of the island, until many years later, they begin to fight again over adjacent land. The more innovative tribal chief, that is, the one who was first to move to the new island, sits down with his senior warriors and ponders what to do, since none are very keen to move to yet another island. They decide that the only two options are (Figure 8.2):

1 Attack and go relentlessly for the enemy's territory.

2 Settle for a smaller part of the island and build on it an impregnable fortress.

Figure 8.2 Competitive strategy against larger companies

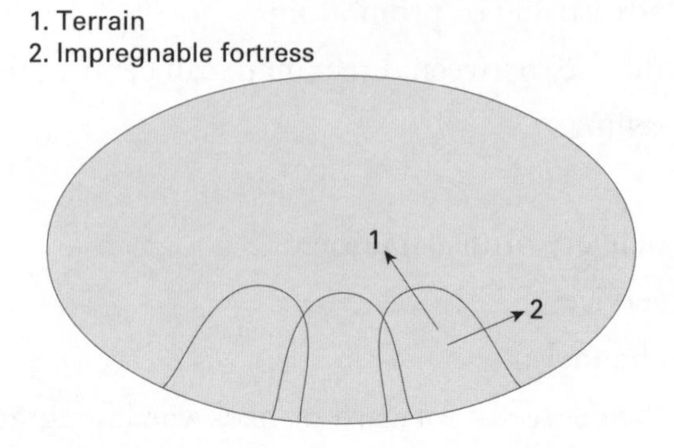

Let's look in turn at each of these options, continuing for a moment longer with the military analogy, and starting with terrain.

Imagine two armies facing each other on a field of battle (depicted by circles). One army has 15 soldiers in it, the other 12. Imagine also that they face each other with rifles and all fire one shot at the other at the same time, also that they don't all aim at the same soldier! Figure 8.3 depicts the progress of each side in disposing of the other. It will be seen that after only three volleys, the army on the right has only one soldier remaining, whilst the army on the left, with eight soldiers remaining, is still a viable fighting unit.

Figure 8.3 The importance of market share

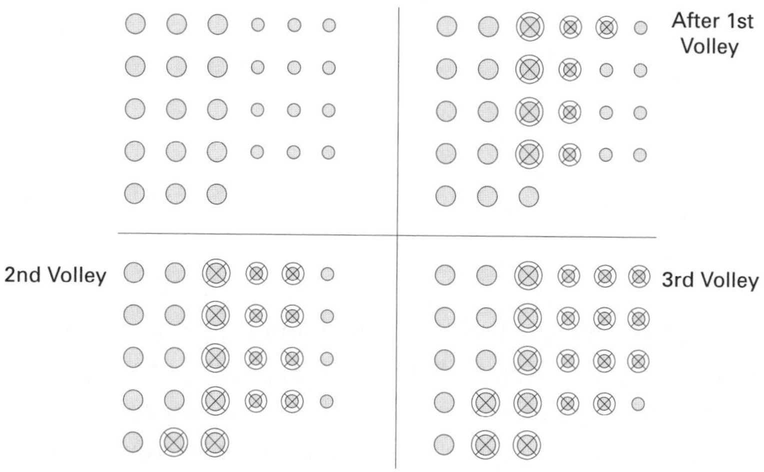

After 1st Volley

2nd Volley

3rd Volley

One interesting fact about this story is that the effect observed here is geometric rather than arithmetic, and is a perfect demonstration of the effect of size and what happens when all things are equal except size. The parallel in industry, of course, is market share.

All things being equal, a company with a larger market share than another should win when competing against a smaller competitor. Or *should* it? Clearly, this is not inevitable, providing the smaller company takes evasive action. Even better, small companies can successfully attack much larger ones, especially given the power that technology has given to SMEs.

The David and Goliath story is repeated every day in the 21st century.

Without repeating the whole history of the Battle of Trafalgar, let me summarize how Nelson won a famous 'David and Goliath' victory over an enemy with superior numbers. (In order to make the point, I have summarized the battle in some fictional numbers – see Figure 8.4.) From this you will see that the enemy had 50 ships against Nelson's 40 ships. What Nelson did was to split his ships into two groups of 16 and one of 8. The 8 ships attacked the centre of the 50 so that Nelson's 32 ships could attack the enemy's 25. They then re-joined what was left of their own 8 and finished off the enemy.

Figure 8.4 Nelson's strength in fewer numbers at the Battle of Trafalgar

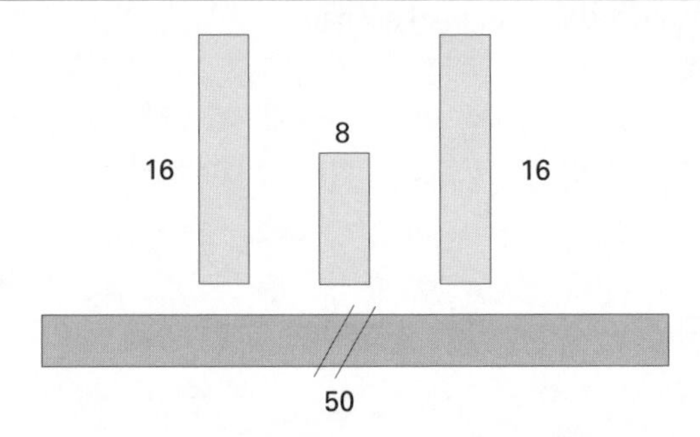

Yes, of course, this is a highly fictional and romanticized version of what really happened. Nonetheless, it does prove that it is possible to beat a numerically superior enemy with fewer resources.

Here are some very general guidelines to help you think about competitive strategies:

1 Know the terrain on which you are fighting (the market).
2 Know the resources of your enemies (competitive analysis).
3 Do something with determination that the enemy is not expecting.

In respect of this last guideline, the great historian of military strategy, Lanchester, put forward the following equation when applying his findings to industry:

$$\text{Fighting strength} = \text{weapon efficiency} \times (\text{number of troops})^2$$

Let us simplify and summarize this. 'Weapon efficiency' can be elements such as advertising, the sales force, the quality of your products, and so on. '(number of troops)^2' is more difficult to explain, but is similar in concept to Einstein's theory of critical mass:

$$\text{Energy} = \text{mass (velocity of light)}^2$$

$$E = mc^2$$

Let us take as an example the use of the sales force. If your competitor's salesperson calls on an outlet, say, twice a month for six months, he or she will have called 12 times. If your salesperson calls four times a month for six months, he or she will have called 24 times. What Lanchester's Square Law says, however, is that the *effect* is considerably more than twice that of your competitor.

An example of this was the very small competitor Canada Dry's attack on the British mixer market. By training the sales force to a high peak of effectiveness (weapon efficiency), and by focusing on specific market segments and out-calling their much larger rival, they were gradually able to occupy particular parts of the market and then move on to the next, until eventually they gained a significant market share. What would have been foolhardy would have been to tackle Schweppes, the market leader, head on in a major battle. The result would have been similar to the fate of the troops in the Charge of the Light Brigade.

We can now return to a relatively simple method for deciding which of the 4Ps need attention and how to prioritize these.

You will recall that in Chapter 6 I showed you how to analyse the needs of customers in a segment by carrying out a SWOT analysis. I repeat the instructions here as Figure 8.5.

Figure 8.5 Instructions for effective SWOT analysis

1. Identify the Critical Success Factors (CSFs) that influence the customer's decision. There are usually not more than six really important factors.
2. Assign an importance weighting to each CSF so that the weightings for each segment totals 100 per cent.
3. Identify the key competitors for each segment and score performance of your company and each key competitor on a scale of 1 to 10, where 1 = very poor and 10 = excellent. Limit to a few competitors (between 1 and 3).
4. Multiply the weights by the scores and add up the weighted score for each competitor.
5. Assess your relative strength by dividing your score by the best competitor's score.
6. Identify the key issues from the analysis.
7. Note that you can change your relative business strength by focusing on improving your strength on the criteria that matter most to customers.

Item 7 in Figure 8.5 is the key to setting strategies for achieving your objectives and an example is given as Figure 8.6.

Figure 8.6 Strategies: revisit CSF scores

CSFs	Weights	Score/weighting Score out of 10 – multiplying these by the weight			
		You	Compet A	Compet B	Compet C
1. Price	50	6 / 3.0	8 / 4.0		
2. Features	25	8 / 2.0	7 / 1.8		
3. Service	15	7 9 / 1.1 1.3	8 / 1.2		
4. Reliability	10	6 / 0.6	5 / 0.5		
5.					
6.					
Totals	100	6.7 6.9	7.5		

Relative Business Strength: –0.8 (current) –0.6 (strategy)

In this fictional example, the service score has been increased from 7 to 9. In reality, when completing your own plans, you would increase firstly those CSFs with the highest weights and those that would result in the greatest improvement in your competitiveness. If you had been doing what I have recommended in Chapter 6, you can now proceed to set strategies for each of your important segments, or products for markets. You can use Figure 8.7 to detail these strategies, work out how much they are going to cost you and who is going to be responsible for carrying out the necessary changes.

This is a relatively simple method for ensuring robust strategies to meet your objectives based on rational analysis.

Figure 8.7 Template for strategy details

Product-market: ______________________	
CSF: ____________ Scores: _____ (current) _______ (objective)	
Description of strategy	
Actions to achieve strategy	
Responsibility	
Approximate cost	

Actions

Amend the scores in your earlier SWOT analyses using Figure 8.6 as an example of how to do this.

A step-by-step strategic planning system

09

By the end of this chapter, you will be able to:

- Prepare your full strategic plan for what you sell and to whom
- Find out why your chosen customers will prefer to buy from you rather than from someone else with something similar to sell
- Prepare a more detailed plan for implementing the first year of your strategy

Introduction

Before setting out the strategic plan, I have a number of important summary points that will act as a reminder of all the crucial messages shared with you throughout this book. The following 10 guidelines summarize most of the intended wisdom set out in the pages of this book.

The Malcolm McDonald 10 Guidelines for World Class Marketing (summary)

1. Understand that marketing is the driver of strategy in the boardroom.
2. Understand your market and how it works.
3. Carry out proper, needs-based segmentation on decision makers.
4. Understand your own strengths and weaknesses.

5 Understand your portfolio of segments.
6 Set realistic objectives and strategies for each segment to grow your sales and profits.
7 Focus and play to win in a few segments only.
8 Calculate whether your objectives and strategies will create shareholder value.
9 Financially justify investments in marketing.
10 Be professional and ethical.

1. Understand that marketing is the driver of strategy in the boardroom

- It is NOT promotion.
- Everything an organization does from R&D through to delivery adapts to and converges on the business value proposition that is projected to the customer.

2. Understand your market and how it works

- Define the market in terms of needs, not products.
- Map how it works from end to end, showing product/service flows in total and your shares.
- Understand how it is changing.
- Identify major junctions where decisions are made.

3. Carry out proper, needs-based segmentation on decision makers

- Do not confuse needs-based segmentation with descriptors such as socio-economics, demographics, geodemographics and psychographics.
- List what is bought (including applications, where and when it is bought).
- List who buys.
- List why they buy.
- Group those with similar needs.

4. Understand your own strengths and weaknesses

- For each segment, list their needs and the relative importance of each (weights).
- Score out of 10 how you and each of our major competitors meet these needs.
- List the external opportunities and threats for each segment.
- List the major issues that need to be addressed for each segment.

5. Understand your portfolio of segments

- Classify on a four box matrix each segment according to its potential for growth in your profits over the planning period (the vertical axis).
- Classify each segment according to your relative strength in each (the horizontal axis).
- This will position each segment as follows:
  - Less attractive segments where you have strengths (1).
  - More attractive segments where you have strengths (2).
  - More attractive markets where you have few strengths (3).
  - Less attractive markets where you have few strengths (4).

6. Set realistic objectives and strategies for each segment to grow your sales and profits

- Set clear priorities and stick to them. You cannot be all things to all customers.
- For quadrant 1, manage for sustained earnings.
- For quadrant 2, manage for growth in revenue and profits.
- For quadrant 3, elect the most promising segments and invest for improving your competitive position. Do NOT try to maximize your profits in these segments.
- For quadrant 4, manage for case and minimize costs.

7. Focus and play to win in a few segments only

- Develop a winning offer for each.
- Quantity the value proposition (creating advantage, not just avoiding disadvantage).
- Become the best in your chosen segments.

8. Calculate whether your objectives and strategies will create shareholder value

- Carry out risk assessment on each strategy in each segment.
- Calculate risk-adjusted net free cash flows for each segment over the planning period.
- Allocate the relative capital employed multiplied by the cost of capital for each segment.
- An overall surplus means that the plan is creating shareholder value.

9. Financially justify investments in marketing

- Measure the indirect impact on sales and profits of all marketing expenditure.
- Measure the impact of promotional expenditure using econometric models.
- Measure and report to the board that your risk-adjusted marketing strategy creates shareholder value.

10. Be professional and ethical

- Develop professional marketing skills.
- If possible, get qualified like other professions.
- Be innovative and open-minded.
- Be ethical at all times and consider the impact of your actions on all stakeholders.

These 10 guidelines can be summarized even further (see Figures 9.1 and 9.2, and Table 9.1).

Figure 9.1 Six ways to develop a winning strategy

1. Define your market in terms of needs, not products. Know how it works from end to end.
2. At decision points, do proper needs-based segmentation.
3. Carry out a detailed SWOT analysis on each segment.
4. Categorize the resulting segments according to the potential of each for you to grow your profits over the next three to five years and according to your relative strength in each compared with your competitors.
5. Focus and play to win in the one or two best segments from item 4 above.
6. Set only a few priorities, involve your team and don't try to be all things to all people.

Figure 9.2 How to become a very profitable leader

1. Identify a profitable, under-served segment (niche).
2. Target only one segment at a time.
3. Create an irresistible offer. Offer quantitative proof that you are the best.
4. Become the obvious expert in your niche.
5. Create a hit list of customers you want to win. Concentrate your firepower.
6. Get high-quality referrals.

Table 9.1 Six tips for competing with bigger companies

1. STUDY	Find their strengths and especially their weaknesses. Know everything about them, especially what their customers don't like.
2. NICHE	Spot one thing they haven't thought about and fill the gap.
3. SURPRISE	Never attack their points of strength (David and Goliath).
4. WORK HARD	Enthusiasm, commitment, energy and, above all, perseverance, eg more attention to instant customer service.
5. BE SMALL	Be small, but above all, be professional, not amateurish.
6. PLAN AHEAD	Develop your strategy (doing the right things). The above tactics will ensure success (doing things right). Plan for the future, not just for this year.

Strategic planning forms

It is, of course, possible to complete the forms provided without reading this book, but I stress that this is very risky and may well lead to a plan without any real substance. Consequently, I refer readers back to the relevant sections of the main text.

Let us remind ourselves that the overall purpose of marketing and its principal focus is the identification and creation of sustainable competitive advantage and that marketing planning is simply a logical sequence and a series of activities leading to the setting of marketing objectives and the formulation of plans for achieving them.

Why marketing planning is necessary

Marketing planning is necessary because of:

- Increasing turbulence, complexity and competitiveness.
- The speed of technological change.
- The need for *you*
  - to help identify sources of competitive advantage;
  - to force an organized approach to develop specificity;
  - to ensure consistent relationships.
- The need for *superiors*
  - to inform.
- The need for *non-marketing functions*
  - to get support.
- The need for *subordinates*
  - to get resources;
  - to gain commitment;
  - to set objectives and strategies.

What should appear in the strategic marketing plan?

Form 1

Figure 9.3 Form 1

Summary of financial projections

This is the first item to appear in the marketing plan.

Its purpose is to summarize for the person reading the plan the financial results over the full three-year planning period. It should be presented as a simple diagram along the following lines.

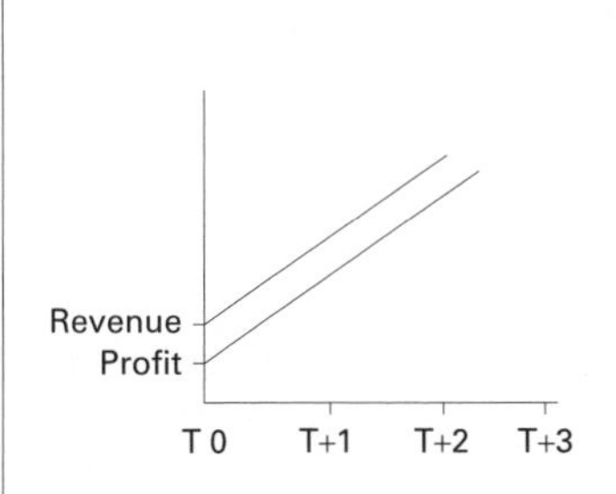

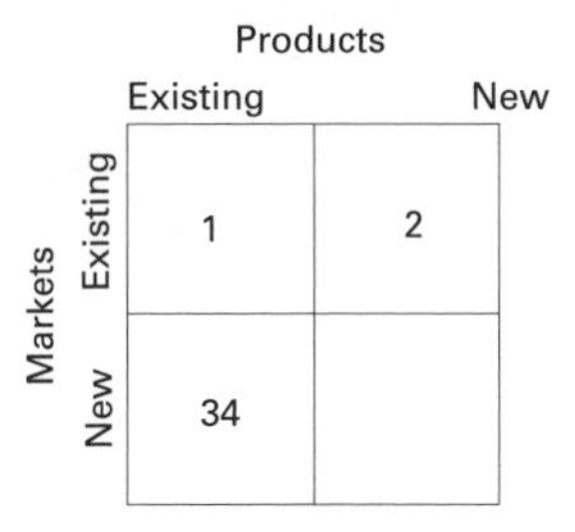

Key (revenue and profit growth)

1. from productivity by product for market for existing products from existing markets
2. from new products in existing markets
3. from existing products in new markets
4. from new products in new markets

This should be accompanied by a brief commentary. For example:

'This three-year business plan shows an increase in revenue from 700,000 euros to 900,000 euros and an increase in contribution from 100,000 euros to 200,000 euros. The purpose of this strategic plan is to show how these increases will be achieved.'

Form 2

Figure 9.4 Form 2

Market overview (with 'market map', if appropriate, together with implications for the organization). Details of how to complete this section are provided in Chapter 5.

It is also helpful if the principal segments can be described here.

- Market definition
- Market map showing vol/rev flows from supplier through to end user, with major decision points highlighted
- Where appropriate, provide a future market map
- Include commentary/conclusions/implications for the company
- At major decision points, include key segments

Form 3

Figure 9.5 Form 3: Strategic marketing planning exercise (SWOT analysis)

1. SEGMENT DESCRIPTION
It should be a *specific* part of the business and should be *very important* to the organization.

2. CRITICAL SUCCESS FACTORS
In other words, how do customers choose?

1	
2	
3	
4	
5	

3. WEIGHTING
How important is each of these CSFs? Score out of 100.

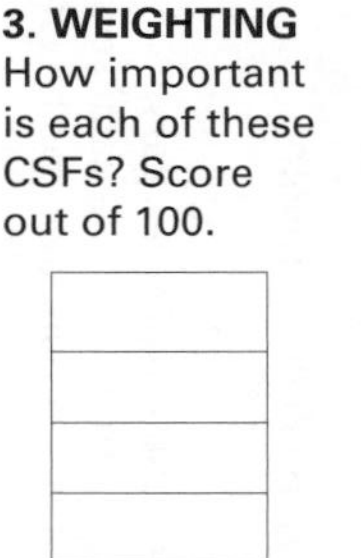

Total 100

4. STRENGTHS/WEAKNESSES ANALYSIS
How would your customers score you and each of your main competitors out of 10 on each of the CSFs? Multiply the score by the weight.

	You	Comp A	Comp B	Comp C	Comp D
1					
2					
3					
4					
5					
°					

5. OPPORTUNITIES/THREATS
What are the few things outside your direct control that have had, and will have, an impact on this part of your business?

OPPORTUNITIES

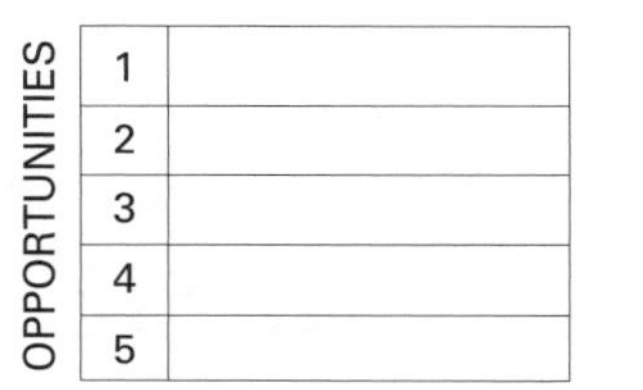

1	
2	
3	
4	
5	

THREATS

6. KEY ISSUES THAT NEED TO BE ADDRESSED
What are the really key issues from the SWOT that need to be addressed?

Form 4

Figure 9.6 Form 4: Portfolio summary of the SWOTs

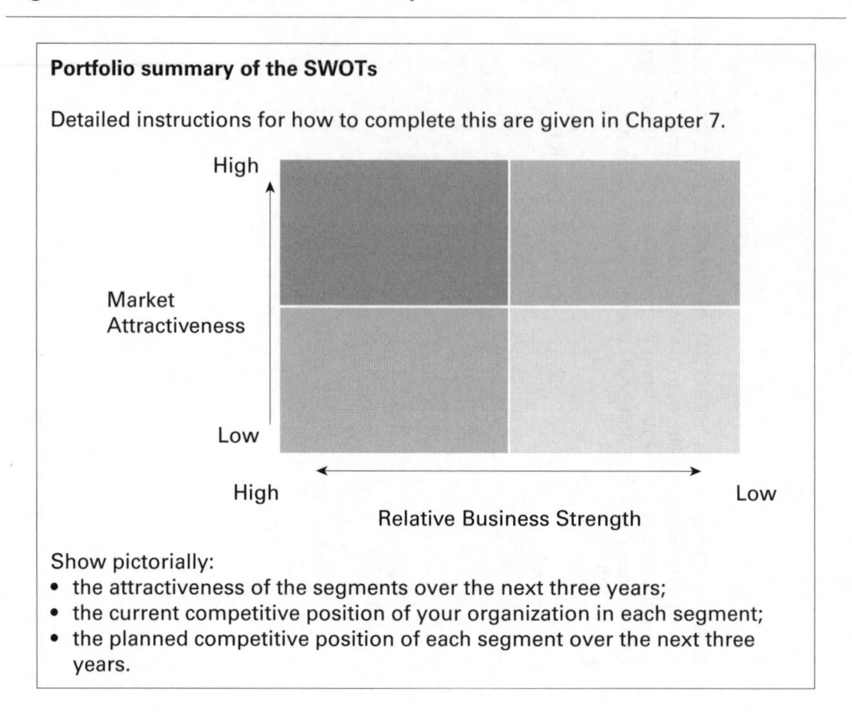

Portfolio summary of the SWOTs

Detailed instructions for how to complete this are given in Chapter 7.

Show pictorially:

- the attractiveness of the segments over the next three years;
- the current competitive position of your organization in each segment;
- the planned competitive position of each segment over the next three years.

Form 5

Figure 9.7 Form 5

Assumptions

Overall, assumptions should be few in number. If the plan can happen irrespective of the assumption, it should not be included.

Form 6

Figure 9.8 Form 6

Marketing objectives and strategies for the next 3 years

- Include objectives (volume, value, market share, profit, as appropriate) for the next 3–5 years for each segment as represented by the planned position of each circle on the SPM
- Include strategies (the 4XPs) with costs for each objective.

Summary of marketing objectives and strategies

Key market segments (list) Summarize remaining market segments as 'other'	Last year (T-1)			Current year (T0)			Planning period (T+3)			Principal marketing strategies (describe)	Cost of marketing strategies
	Vol/ val%	market share%	gross margin	Vol/ val%	market share%	gross margin	Vol/ val%	market share%	gross margin		

Form 7

Figure 9.9 Form 7

Summary (in words and numbers) of main marketing objectives and strategies

Form 8

Figure 9.10 Form 8

Consolidated budget for the next three years
This will be a consolidation of all the revenues, costs and profits for the next 3 years and should accord with the financial summary provided earlier

Financial projections for three years
Financial projections for the full planning period should be provided under all the principal standard revenue and cost headings as specified by your organization

Your strategic plan is complete and you can now proceed to prepare a more detailed specification of actions for the first year of the plan.

The one-year marketing plan

(This should be kept separate from the three-year strategic plan and should not be completed until the three-year plan has been approved.)

Specific sub-objectives for products and segments, supported by more detailed strategy and action statements, should now be developed. Here, include *budgets* and *forecasts* and a *consolidated budget*. These must reflect the marketing objectives and strategies, and in turn the objectives, strategies and programmes must reflect the agreed budgets and sales forecasts. Their main purpose is to delineate the major steps required in implementation, to assign accountability, to focus on the major decision points, and to specify the required allocation of resources and their timing.

If the procedures in this system are followed, a hierarchy of *objectives* will be built up in such a way that every item of budgeted expenditure can be related directly back to the initial financial objectives (this is known as task-related budgeting). Thus when, say, advertising has been identified as a means of achieving an objective in a particular market (that is, advertising is a strategy to be used), all advertising expenditure against items appearing in the budget can be related back specifically to a major objective. The essential feature of this is that budgets are set against both the overall marketing objectives and the sub-objectives for each element of the marketing mix. The principal advantage is that this method allows you to build up and demonstrate an increasingly clear picture of your markets. This method of budgeting also allows every item of expenditure to be fully accounted for as part of an objective approach. It also ensures that when changes have to be made during the period to which the plan relates, such changes can be made in a way that causes the least damage to your long-term objectives.

Suggested format for a one-year marketing plan

1 (a) **Overall objectives** (*see Forms 1 and 2 in the one-year marketing plan documentation*) – these should cover the following:

Volume or value, Value last year, Current year estimate, Budget next year

Gross margin, Last year, Current year estimate, Budget next year

Against each there should be few words of commentary/explanation.

(b) **Overall strategies** – eg new customers, new products, advertising, sales promotion, selling, customer service, pricing. For a list of marketing strategies, see Chapter 8.

2 (a) **Sub-objectives** (see *Form 3 in the one-year marketing plan documentation*) – more detailed objectives should be provided for products, or markets, or segments, or major customers, as appropriate.

(b) **Strategies** – the means by which sub-objectives will be achieved should be stated.

(c) **Action/tactics** – the details, timing, responsibility and cost should also be stated.

3 Summary of marketing activities and costs (*see Form 4 in the one-year marketing plan documentation*).

4 Contingency plan (*see Form 5 in the one-year marketing plan documentation*) – it is important to include a contingency plan, which should address the following questions:

(a) What are the critical assumptions on which the one-year plan is based?

(b) What would the financial consequences be (ie the effect on the operating income) if these assumptions did not come true? For example, if a forecast of revenue is based on the assumption that a decision will be made to buy new plant by a major customer, what would the effect be if that customer did not go ahead?

(c) How will these assumptions be measured?

(d) What action will you take to ensure that the adverse financial effects of an unfulfilled assumption are mitigated, so that you end up with the same forecast profit at the end of the year?

To measure the risk, assess the negative or downside, asking what can go wrong with each assumption that would change the outcome. For example, if a market growth rate of 5 per cent is a key assumption, what lower growth rate would have to occur before a substantially different management decision would be taken? For a capital project, this would be the point at which the project would cease to be economical.

5 Operating result and financial ratios (*see Form 6 in the one-year marketing plan documentation*). **Note:** This form is provided only as an example, for, clearly, all organizations will have their own formats – this should include:

- Net revenue
- Gross margin

- Adjustments
- Marketing costs
- Administration costs
- Interest
- Operating result
- ROS
- ROI

6 **Key activity planner** (*see Form 7 in the one-year marketing plan documentation*) – finally, you should summarize the key activities and indicate the start and finish. This should help you considerably with monitoring the progress of your annual plan.

7 **Other** – there may be other information you wish to provide, such as sales call plans.

Form 1

Table 9.2 Form 1

Overall objectives				
Product/market/ segment/ application/ customer	Volume	Value	Gross margin	Commentary
	(T–1) (T0) (T+1)	(T–1) (T0) (T+1)	(T–1) (T0) (T+1)	

Form 2

Table 9.3 Form 2

Overall strategies		
	Strategies	**Cost**
1		
2		
3		
4		
5		
6		
7		
8		
9		
10		
Comments		

Form 3

Table 9.4 Form 3

Sub-objectives, strategies, actions, responsibilities, timing, cost						
Product/market/ Segment/ application/ Customer	**Objective**	**Strategies**	**Action**	**Responsibility**	**Timing**	**Cost**

Form 4

Table 9.5 Form 4

	T-1	T 0	T+1	Comments
Depreciation Salaries Postage/telephone Stationery Legal and professional Training Data processing Advertising Sales promotion Travelling and entertaining Exhibitions Printing Meetings/conferences Market research Internal costs Other (specify)				
Total				

Form 5

Table 9.6 Form 5

Suggested downside risk assessment format						
Key assumption	**Basis of assumption**	**What event would have to happen to make this strategy unattractive?**	**Risk of such an event occurring**	**Impact if event occurs**	**Trigger point for action**	**Actual contingency Action proposal**

Form 6

Table 9.7 Form 6

	(T – 1)	(T 0)	(T + 1)
Net revenue Gross margin Adjustments Marketing costs Administration costs Interest			
Operating result			
Other internet and financial costs			
Result after financial costs			
Net result			

Form 7

Table 9.8 Form 7

Key activity planner												
Date/ activity	Jan	Feb	Mar	Apr	May	Jun	Jul	Aug	Sep	Oct	Nov	Dec

Final comments

Armed with the tangible results of this wisdom you have captured in the strategic and tactical plans, you can face the future with confidence.

Best of luck!

However, in case it doesn't all go exactly to plan, I do have some further brief guidelines in Chapter 10.

How to deal with adversity 10

For the entrepreneur in all businesses and particularly in start-ups and SMEs, adversity is not a risk; it's a fact. I liken adversity to the stepping stones to success – one step back and three steps forward. If you have not experienced adversity in business you have almost certainly failed to achieve your potential. It has always been a necessity for real success. Talk to 10 successful people and nine will tell you about their struggles and failures first.

My experience in business has been to face up to adversity with a cheerful and positive frame of mind, no matter how worrying. Taking time to think through the cause provided the strength and inspiration to come back stronger with new and better ideas rather than being weighed down by them. So facing challenges can be a positive experience that promotes perseverance, motivation, determination and strength of character to overcome them – the stuff required of entrepreneurs.

I have learned that the emotional intensity of failure provides a stimulus for reflection and further knowledge acquisition. It provides an opportunity to re-examine and re-evaluate your previous decisions, to help you to learn how to become open to challenges, accept mistakes and commit to the learning process at each setback – and when you have your next success, you will have an awesome story to tell!

It was not always thus, as other crisis times have come along to test my nerve and resilience, not often as a result of my own deficiencies but nevertheless ones that had to be overcome to survive. For example, businesses are built by people and are often destroyed by them also, not just events, so I have found choosing the right partners who share my vision and passion and are prepared, like me – despite the problems – to get things done, is one of the main secrets of success.

In real times of adversity many problems and difficulties arise all at the same time, some real, some imagined and a technique I have perfected with time and experience is to 'box' those I can do nothing to influence at the time, put them out of the reach of my mind and it is amazing how many go away or resolve themselves by just pressing on. They will, of course, eventually have to be dealt with and you will need to put some time into thinking through the consequences for you and your company.

I have come to recognize that failure and adversities are almost a daily routine. Geniuses are rarely born. They emerge by refining their raw talent though regular practice and working through new ideas to get it right, as only then can great ideas turn into great performances and success stories.

When I lost my job as a main board director of a fast-moving consumer goods company some 38 years ago – I was lucky it wasn't my fault – I initially experienced a deep depression, wondering how on earth I would be able to provide for my family.

I soon shook myself out of this trough of despair, however, as it was clear to me that I would have to help myself to recover and that no one else was going to come forward with some kind of magic wand.

I started by listing all my positives and all my negatives. I resolved to improve as many of the negatives as possible and to use the positives to my advantage. I had to be crystal clear about what I wanted, so I wrote down my objectives systematically, with time frames for achievement against each. I then wrote down what I had to do next week, next month, by the end of the year, next year, the next five years and the next 10 years. It was the very act of writing down all this stuff that motivated me to get out of bed each day to tackle my 'To Do' lists.

Strangely enough, one of my goals was to start a successful SME, something I achieved quite quickly. I 'invented' a process I called 'The Marketing Audit', and licensed it to other consultants.

I used this as my springboard to join a business school (Cranfield School of Management) to do a PhD, then became a lecturer, Senior

Lecturer, Professor and Deputy Director of the School, all in the relatively short time of 15 years, whilst still running three of my own SMEs and being Chairman of five others.

Would that the above fairy-tale story was as trouble-free as I have made it sound. There were many times of adversity, but as I said in my opening paragraph above, each problem and setback can be best tackled by facing up to it and, above all, being determined to learn from it.

In this book I have explained how you can develop a winning strategy to grow your sales and profits. My processes work, as I have proved many times over my 60-year career. Combining these with my advice about adversity is a magical formula for success. Today at 77, I still advise the operating boards of many of the world's best companies, am a professor at five of the UK's top business schools, have written 46 books, and continue to enjoy life with family and friends. Luckily, they all say to me, 'You look well!'

INDEX

Note: page numbers in *italics* indicate Figures or Tables.